"十三五"普通高等教育核心规划教材

主　审　王守仁
总主编　张绍杰　魏承杰

U1020449

新时代主题大学英语
NEW ERA THEME-BASED COLLEGE ENGLISH

基础英语写作

Foundation-Based English Writing

学生用书

主　编　马建华　张　飞
编　者　王　丽　赵丽娜　赵立书　庞　博

中国人民大学出版社
·北京·

“新时代主题大学英语”系列教材编委会

主　　审　王守仁

总 主 编　张绍杰　魏承杰

编 委 会　顾世民　高　长　郭英剑　胡艳玲　刘白玉　李丹莉　鲁修红
刘　爽　刘夏青　李秀梅　李永强　刘　志　李京廉　刘　瑾
马建华　苗兴伟　潘春静　史光达　隋晓冰　孙卓夫　魏承杰
王明新　王守仁　文　旭　王　卓　谢世坚　王慧敏　杨连瑞
杨冬玲　袁凤识　曾洪伟　张　飞　张　清　杨翠艳　张焕芹
张绍杰　周晓玲　朱小琳　郑　禹　陈国兴

总 策 划　鞠方安

执行策划　黄　婷　程子姝　吴振良

总序

FOREWORD

我国的大学英语教学在改革开放40余年的发展历程中砥砺前行，成就斐然。站在新时代的起点上，大学英语的教与学需要与时俱进，不断探索，再上新台阶，开辟新境界。

在时代的感召下，中国人民大学出版社邀请张绍杰教授和魏承杰教授主编一套新的大学英语教材，同时邀请我担任教材的主审。作为读者先睹为快，我认为本套教材有以下特色。

第一，提出了独到的编写理念。一套好的教材，往往都有其与众不同的编写理念以及这种编写理念背后的理论支撑。**本套教材编者根据二语习得有关“知识学习”的理论定识（assumptions），深入思考外语教学过程中知识和能力的关系问题，提出了“外语显性知识技能化”和“外语技能隐性知识化”的教学理念并以此作为编写指导思想。**在我国以往的外语教学实践中，我们时而过分重视外语知识的传授和学习而忽视与能力培养相关的技能训练，时而过分重视技能的训练而忽视知识的传授和学习。由于不能正确认识和处理二者的关系，导致外语教学和学习效果不佳。**本套教材所提出的教学理念，揭示了外语教学过程就是帮助外语学习者通过目标语的显性知识学习，继而形成外语技能，再通过外语技能的训练转化为隐性知识进而形成外语能力的规律，更加合理地解释了知识和能力二者相互作用、互为转化的关系。我认为，这一理念突出了大学英语课程目标的工具性特点，既有对我国外语教学传统的传承，也有对当今外语教学观念的汲取，可谓“守正出新”，十分契合我国大学英语教与学的实际情况，有理论上的创新，值得大家重视。**

第二，突出“以学生学习为中心”理念。以学生学习为中心（learning-centered）理念标志着传统外语教学转向现代外语教学在方法上的变革。本套教材将“以学生学习为中心”理念贯穿于教材的设计之中，不仅体现在针对广大英语学习者的知识和学习需求选择知识内容，而且体现在这些知识内容与能力培养的有机结合。例如，主体教材《综合教程》、《写作教程》和《视听说教程》都注重知识呈现的系统性，避免知识学习的碎片化。教材中的知识内容包含词汇知识、语法知识、语用知识、阅读知识、翻译知识、文化知识等，构成较为系统的知识体系。根据学生的实际情况，教师可对这些知识内容有选择地教，学生也可根据自己的情况有选择地学，甚至无师自通。为了指导学生循序渐进地学习，《综合教程》按两大板块设计：基础性学习（foundation-based learning）和探索性学习（exploration-oriented learning）。前者重在语言知识、阅读知识、翻译知识的学习，突出通用英语基础知识的夯实和基本语言技能的提高；后者重在语用知识（包括语篇知识、修辞知识、文化知识）的学习，突出语言的应用及高阶技能的训练，旨在提升学习者的语用能力、思辨能力，以及培养跨语言文化意识的人文素养。“基础性学习”和“探索性学习”平行设计，相得益彰，体现了“以学生学习为中心”的理念，成为本套教材的一大亮点。此外，本套教材顺应网络时代对英语学习者读写能力提出的新要求，包含了《写作教程》（共四册），将阅读与写作有机结合，满足英语学习者提高读写能力的不同需求。“重读写”是我国外语教学长期以来形成的传统，新时代大学英语教学应坚持并弘扬这一立足中国国情的外语教学优良传统。在培养和发展学生的英语读写能力方面，本套教材可谓另辟蹊径、大胆创新。

第三，实现思想性和主题性的有机统一。教育的目的是培养人，必须坚持立德树人的根本导向。在如何满足立德树人的内在要求方面，本套教材提供了范例。具体来说，就是严格把握题材内容的思想性，引导学生树立正确的人生观、世界观和价值观，春风化雨，润物无声，寓育人于教学过程之中。本套教材围绕八大主题遴选题材，贴近大学生的生活，中外风土人情交融，话题喜闻乐见，语言生动且内容丰富，有真实感和时代感。这些主题题材的内容不仅体现人类对真善美的共同追求，体现人类对社会生活的积极态度和信念以及对未来美好生活的憧憬，而且体现中国文化、中国故事和中国精神，有机渗透社会主义核心价值观。本套教材融思想性和主题性为一体，有助于培育学生的中国情怀，拓展其国际视野。

本套教材无论是从编写理念到整体设计，还是从教学内容的选定到练习项目的编排，都体现出自主研发的本土化教材特色，对当今大学英语教材的编写具有引领作用。我认为，本套教材适合中国学生的实际状况和需求，朝着好学、好教、好用的期待目标迈出了坚实的一步。

宝剑锋从磨砺出，梅花香自苦寒来。大学英语教材的研发实属不易，两位总主编张绍杰教授和魏承杰教授带领本套教材的研发团队孜孜以求、精益求精，他们这种追求精品、打造品牌的精神令我钦佩。我期待本套教材在使用中不断完善，为我国的大学英语教学做出应有的贡献。

是为序。

主审　王守仁
南京大学人文社会科学资深教授
2019 年 3 月

总前言

PREFACE

大学英语教学伴随我国改革开放40余年不断改进、创新、发展。为适应新时代大学英语教学的需要，借振兴本科教育之国策，承《大学英语教学指南》(新版)(以下简称《指南》)之精神，乘《中国英语能力等级量表》颁布之东风，我们研发了本套“新时代主题大学英语”系列教材。现就这套教材的结构设计、使用对象、编写目的、编写理念、教材特色、教师发展这六个方面阐述如下，以飨用者。

1. 结构设计

本套教材为大学英语课程通用英语系列教材，按照培养英语应用能力总体目标设计。本套教材由以下四个品种构成。

《综合教程》(配教师用书)	基础篇、1~4册
《视听说教程》(配教师用书)	基础篇、1~4册
《进阶快速阅读》	1~4册
《写作教程》(配教师用书)	1~4册

其中，《综合教程》的词汇量以高中毕业的要求为起点，对选材进行科学的控制；其知识的安排遵循由易到难、由简到繁的原则。《进阶快速阅读》按照快速阅读要求编写，其阅读速度、阅读理解率、阅读效率等可根据书中独具匠心设计的三种表格进行即时自测，为师生提供科学、完整、系统的有效数据；《视听说教程》将听说有机结合，按先输入后输出的规律编写；《写作教程》将阅读与写作结合，遵循从词句到篇章，再从实用文体到学术文体，直至综合测试的顺序编排。

2. 使用对象

大学英语课程不同于其他通识课程，如何面向各级各类高校水平参差不齐的英语学习者，本套教材对此做了精心设计安排。首先，针对入学水平较低的学生专门设计了基础篇教材；其次，主体教材的设计融大学英语教学基础目标和提高目标为一体，适合二本和三本院校使用；同时还设计了基于提高目标的知识内容和任务模块，适合一本院校(包括目前的“双一流”院校)使用。因此，**本套教材适用对象宽泛，结构设计别具匠心，可供不同院校大学英语教学选用。**

3. 编写目的

课程与教材是教育教学的基础性教学资源。改革开放40余年以来，大学英语课程与时俱进，教材建设成绩显著，但尚不能满足各级、各类高等学校大学英语教学之需求，更难以满足存有地域差异、水平差异、个体差异的大学英语学习者之需求。本科教育处在人才培养的核心地位、教育教学的基础地位、新时代教育发展的前沿地位。大学英语课程，作为本科通识教育的重要组成部分，具有不可替代的功能，它在大学通识教育中发挥其独特作用。本套教材顺应新时代要求，为大学英语教育教学提供新的教学资源。

《指南》是大学英语教学的指针，引导大学英语教学的方向，亦是教材编写的重要依据。《指南》将大学英语课程分为三类，即通用英语课程、专门用途英语课程和跨文化交际课程。**本套通用大学英语教材，秉持“推陈出新”“探求新知”之精神，贯彻落实《指南》之要求，举多校之力、博采众长，融入新理念、新目标、新要求而设计编写，旨在满足新时代背景下大学英语教学的需要。**

4. 编写理念

本套教材基于二语习得有关“知识学习”的理论定识（assumptions），遵循“外语显性知识技能化”和“外语技能隐性知识化”的教学理念编写。人类知识区分为显性知识 (explicit knowledge) 和隐性知识 (tacit knowledge) 两种知识形态。显性知识是关于事实和原理的知识，隐性知识是关于行动和信息来源的知识。简单地说，显性知识是可编码和言传的客观性知识，而隐性知识是不可或不易编码的意会的个体内化的知识，只有将显性知识转化为隐性知识才能发挥人的主观能动性和创造性。将知识学习理论应用于外语学习的相关研究表明，显性知识是有意识的知识，对语言使用起监控作用，学习者对语言形式的注意程度决定语言输入在多大程度上转化为摄入 (intake)，有意识的语言操练可促进显性知识向隐性知识的转化；隐性知识是潜意识的知识，有助于语言使用的自动化，理解性输入可产生隐性知识，而隐性知识的发展决定着学习者自主使用语言的能力发展。

二语习得有关知识学习的理论揭示了外语学习中目标语知识和语言能力发展的内在联系和相互作用。**“外语显性知识技能化”和“外语技能隐性知识化”的理念，体现了外语教学过程就是帮助外语学习者通过目标语的显性知识学习形成外语技能的过程，再通过外语技能的训练转化成隐性知识进而形成外语能力的过程。**“外语显性知识技能化”的过程，指通过基于外语知识学习的训练转化为外语技能的过程；而“外语技能隐性知识化”的过程，是指通过技能的训练使知识内化形成隐性知识从而促进外语能力发展的过程。因此，我们将这种知识与技能互相转化的定识作为统领本套教材的编写理念。主要基于如下三点考量：

首先，基于对我国高校庞大群体的英语学习者高中阶段英语实际水平的考量。大学英语四级考试显示，每年有平均2/3的考生考试成绩达不到规定的及格分数线，表现为英语基本功不扎实，语言知识尚未转化为语言能力。即使“双一流”大学的考生通过考试，其使用英语表达的应用能力也非常薄弱。其次，《指南》明确提出要培养大学英语学习者的“英语应用能力”。这是针对大学英语课程的工具性而提出的，它既包括提高大学生的听、说、读、写、译的能力，也包括获得在学术或职业领域使用专门用途英语进行交流的能力。应用能力突出强调了使用英语进行表达和交流的能力，这种能力的培养有赖于对英语显性知识的技能化和英语技能的知识化过程。再次，英语学习者的语言行为中存在大量负迁移 (negative transfer) 现象，原因主要在于英语学习者目标语的语言意识 (language awareness) 匮乏，也从另一方面证明，英语学习者获得英语应用能力依赖于对英语显性语言知识的掌握。因此，**大学英语学习者的现状和水平反映出，语言知识不是要不要教，而是教什么语言知识和怎么教语言知识。**本套教材正是根据上述编写理念，围绕知识学习和技能培养做了精心设计和安排，在传承教材编写传统范式的基础上推陈出新。

5. 教材特色

本套教材遵循二语 / 外语学习规律的教学理念，体现学科知识的相对完整性、系统性和时代性。《综合教程》突出对英语显性知识的系统学习和掌握、对各类语篇的理解，以及对基本技能的综合训练；《视听说教程》注重在真实情景下对听说知识技能的培养和训练；《进阶快速阅读》突出培养快速阅读技能，强化快速阅读知识技能的系统训练；《写作教程》分为《基础英语写作》《实用英语写作》《学术英语写作》《进阶英语写作》，突出写作知识的系统学习和技能培养；此外，《综合教程》和《视听说教程》各设计基础篇一册，供新生入学时英语水平较低的学生使用，以贯彻大学英语教学“分类指导、因材施教”的原则。总体上，本套教材突出强化知识学习和技能训练有机结合的理念。

与同类教材相比，本套教材体现出如下几个方面的特色。

体系设计的创新性：我国拥有世界上最大的英语学习者群体。虽然英语在基础教育阶段已得到广泛的普及，但因我国幅员广阔、区域差别较大、城乡差别明显，大多数英语学习者在考入大学时，其英语水平尚未达到基础阶段课标的要求。针对这一实际情况，为贯彻《指南》倡导的“分类指导、因材施教”的原则，我们设计了《综合教程》和《视听说教程》的基础篇课程，供入大学时英语水平较低的学生选用。这种设计是同类教材中鲜见的，也体现了以学生为本的教育理念。此外，还体现在《进阶快速阅读》的设计上。我们不但增设了新题型，而且根据美国罗格斯大学教授兼阅读中心主任爱德华·弗赖伊的教学理念，精心设计了三个“阅读进程表”，可供师生进行形成性评估。另一个鲜明特点是，设计了由四个分册构成的《写作教程》，将读写有机结合，针对我国英语学习者需要的写作技能进行系统训练，突出写作能力培养在发展英语应用能力中的作用。这样的设计理念不但适应了时代的要求，而且对英语学习者终身学习能力的发展大有裨益。

选材的思想性：本套教材的选材，除了注重题材和体裁的多样性、可读性、语言的时代性、贴近大学生学习和生活之外，更加突出了其思想性。**所谓思想性，就是本套教材文本体现的鲜明的价值观导向。它不仅体现在人类对真善美的共同追求，对社会生活的积极态度和信念以及对未来美好生活的憧憬，对推动社会进步和科学发展的奋斗精神和创新精神，而且体现在教材文本包含着弘扬社会主义**

核心价值观的中国文化元素及中国故事，蕴含着立德树人的价值取向。

学科教育教学中的立德树人不是空洞的说教，而是寓育人于教学过程之中。除了英语教师课堂上应有立德树人的意识外，教材的选材内容起着“细雨润无声”的育人作用。基于这样的理解，我们特别重视教材的选材，对每一篇文本都是从全球化、跨文化、多元化的视角经过严格的筛选，这些文本内容生动、主题鲜活、蕴含丰富，体现思想性和知识性的有机统一。

知识的系统性：我们认为，外语学习者的语言认知能力发展依赖于对目标语语言知识的理解、掌握及内化，只有将外语知识技能化和外语技能知识化，才能使外语学习者具有使用目标语进行建构意义的语言能力。因此，本套教材注重知识呈现的系统性，避免知识的碎片化，或将知识隐含在练习体系中的“去知识化”现象中。这主要体现在主干教材《综合教程》、《写作教程》和《视听说教程》在知识内容选择上，包含词汇知识、语法知识、语用知识、阅读知识、翻译知识、文化知识等，构成教材较为系统的知识体系。例如，《综合教程》按两大板块设计：基础性学习（foundation-based learning）和探索性学习（exploration-oriented learning）。前者重在语言知识、阅读知识、翻译知识的学习，突出通用英语基础知识的夯实和基本语言技能的提高；后者重在语用知识（包括语篇知识、修辞知识、文化知识）的学习，突出语用法的掌握及其高阶技能的训练，提升学习者的语用能力。

目标的工具性：本套教材依据《指南》，以培养学生的英语应用能力为目标而设计。大学英语教学目标分为基础目标、提高目标和发展目标。基础目标是针对大多数非英语专业学生所确定的英语学习基本要求，也是本科生毕业时应达到的基本要求；提高目标是针对那些入学时英语基础较好且有较高学习需求的学生而确定的；发展目标是根据学校人才培养计划的需要以及部分学有余力学生的多元需求确定的。提高目标和发展目标也是为满足那些对英语应用能力有较高要求的专业而确定的。本套教材贯彻《指南》的精神，侧重基础目标的实现，兼顾提高目标，突出外语工具性的特点，主要培养学生的通用英语应用能力。同时，也体现大学英语学习者将外语作为工具的显著特征。

另外，本套教材也兼顾人文性目标的综合素质培养。由于本套教材针对通用英语的基础目标，兼顾提高目标，因而特别突出能力素质，即思辨能力、自主学习能力和语用能力（语篇建构能力、跨文化交流能力、中外文化交流能力）的培养。本套教材还强调，人文性目标的素质培养主要通过两种途径来实现。一是通过选材实现道德素质、思维品质、国际视野、中国情怀等素质的培养。如在不同主题下尽量选择具有思想性、蕴含人的积极价值取向的素材，使学生在悄然的学习过程中受到感染和熏陶。二是通过精心设计问题和任务板块实现能力素质的培养。例如，从知识的系统性设计，到语篇分析的问题与回答，再到语用模块的话题与讨论，以及针对语言文化差异的翻译练习，都体现出培养学生的思辨能力、自主学习能力和语用能力的目的要求。

6. 教师发展

本套教材的使用能否达到既定的教学目标，关键在于教师。因此，我们充分考虑到在使用教材过程中英语教师发展问题。

教学相长：教师发展 (faculty development) 的决定因素，是教师首先要成为一名教师学习者 (teacher learner)。教师应建立终身学习的理念，在教学过程中温故知新，不断提升自身的教学水平。教师伴随教学过程不断增长学科知识、提高教学水平，这是教师发展的基本规律。**本套教材各类品种设有内容全面的《教师用书》（包括参考答案）、精心制作的教学课件、网络平台等教学支持系统，这些设计有利于帮助任课教师掌握课文的教学目的、教学重点、难点；拓展任课教师的知识面和教学技巧；给学生提供科学、准确的问题解答。**

教研相长：教学与研究相辅相成，教学过程可以为教学研究和学科研究发现问题、提出问题，学科研究又可以支撑教学、反哺教学。二者相互作用、相互促进，才能成就一名优秀教师。教师不但要成为教师学习者，而且要成为教师研究者 (teacher researcher)，两种身份建构是教师发展的内在动因。**本套教材提供的知识内容可作为任课教师进一步思考和进行学科研究的领域，**例如：《综合教程》中的用法与使用 (Usage and Use) 板块，涉及语用知识，任课教师可将其作为一个研究领域去深入学习和探索，必定会学有所获、研有所得；针对课文涉及的话题与讨论 (Topics and Discussion)，旨在提高学生的思辨能力，课堂上的讨论可通过录像记录作为研究如何培养思辨能力的素材；《写作教程》的设计为研究外语学习者的写作规律提供实证的基础；翻译练习实践对于探究中英文化的差异提供了丰富的例证。其他配套教材中设置的某些任务都可以作为研究的范围，在此无须一一列举。

诚然，教师发展的另一途径是针对教材组织的各种教师培训活动。我们将根据教师的需求，开展各类教学、教研活动，以促进教师教学水平的提高。

本套教材经过研发团队三年多的艰苦努力，终于出版问世。**这是一套具有体系设计的创新性、编写理念的独特性、选材的思想性、知识的系统性、目标的工具性和人文性等特点的大学英语通用教材，我们的目标是好教、好学、好用。我们期待使用者的检验。**

最后，我们感谢各分册主编及团队成员同舟共济、团结协作，为此套教材的编写付出的辛勤劳动。所有分册主编和编者均是国内高校教学一线的教授和骨干教师，他们对于大学英语课程和教学具有深刻的认知，对于教材研发有着丰富的经验；我们还聘请了多名外籍专家参与部分编写工作和所有教材英语文本的审校。因此确保了本套教材的高质量和适用性。我们特别感谢同人、朋友们在此套教材编写过程中提出的宝贵意见和建议。

鉴于编者的水平及时间有限，教材难免存在不足之处。我们诚邀学界的同行、专家，尤其是辛勤耕耘在一线的英语教师不吝赐教。

总主编　张绍杰　魏承杰

2019 年 3 月

使用说明

《基础英语写作》和《实用英语写作》分别为“新时代主题大学英语”系列教材（本科用）之一，适合各类高校大学英语本科学生基础阶段（大学一、二年级），也包括高职高专的学生使用，可作为一门必修课教材使用，也可作为一门选修课教材选用。

这两册书是遵循读写结合、讲练结合、实用性和系统性兼顾、时代性和可读性统一的原则而编写的一套写作教材，既可以配合《综合英语》使用，也可以单独使用。

一、教材特色

① 关注显性知识和隐性知识的关系，有效提高学习者的写作能力

本套写作教材正确认识显性知识和隐性知识二者之间的关系，开辟显性学习的路径，为系统地学习相关显性语言知识提供理解性输入，创造由显性知识向隐性知识转化的条件；同时，强化有针对性的写作实践，通过实际的任务操练促进显性知识的内化，形成隐性知识，从而掌握写作技巧并最终提高写作能力。

② 尊重语言学习规律，读写结合，提高写作能力

《基础英语写作》和《实用英语写作》都遵循读写结合的编写原则，将阅读与写作知识的理解相结合，通过阅读文本的范例或实例加深对写作知识的消化和理解，达到以读促写的作用。

③ 选材丰富多样，突出话题意识，体现中国元素

选材尽量与本套系列教材的主题大学英语教程（theme-based）保持一致，包括：个人和家庭、学习和就业、交通和旅游、科学与技术、文学与鉴赏、文化与种族、人与社会、情感和思想等。充分考虑了思想性、规范性、时代性、可读性、多样性等几个维度，内容丰富多样，尤其考虑了中国元素，每册至少有两篇反映当代中国的话题。

④ 强化学生中心理念，围绕活动设计教学，提高学生参与度

本教材突破以讲授写作技巧为主的常规教材模式，实现了由“教”向“学”的转变，使教学过程实现由关注“教的目的”向关注“学的需要”转变，形成以教师引导和启发、学生积极主动参与为主要特征的教学常态，以学生学习为中心，在教学活动设计上充分考虑学生的认知水平、心智状况、情感态度等实际情况，提高学生参与的积极性。

二、主要内容与构成

《基础英语写作》和《实用英语写作》供基础阶段使用，每册设置 8 个单元，每个单元包括 A、B 两篇课文，Text A 侧重基础知识和常用技巧，Text B 侧重相关知识的延展。整体结构由 5 个板块构成：Part I Learn from the Text、Part II Learn to Know、Part III Learn to Do、Part IV Learn to Know More 和 Part V Learn to Do More。

（一）编排设计

1 Text A 部分按三大板块编排设计：知识观察（Observation）、知识讲解（Explanation）、知识应用（Application）。知识观察是通过课文阅读和解析引出本单元要讲的知识点，一般为 3~5 个问题，即 Part I Learn from the Text 部分；知识讲解是依据确定的知识点进行解析，例证取之于课文，分析讲解应简明精练，即 Part II Learn to Know 部分；知识应用是针对讲解的知识设计练习或任务活动，练习量一般为 3~5 个操练活动，设计要针对中国英语学习者写作中常遇到的重点、难点问题、常出现的语用失误等，即 Part III Learn to Do 部分。

2 Text B 部分是 Text A 部分知识内容的拓展（Extension）。选材的内容基本与 Text A 部分相关，针对写作知识或技巧的一个方面，至多两个方面，结合课文实例进行拓展讲解和分析。Text B 部分的讲解为知识拓展板块（Extension），讲解后不单设针对性练习，即 Part IV Learn to Know More 部分。

3 Text B 部分后设置 Consolidation 板块练习，操练内容包含 A、B 两部分，体现综合训练。有针对性地考虑改错、命题写作、看图写作、课文缩写、课文概述、仿写、续写这几种类型。这部分可为学习者提供更大的选择空间，即 Part V Learn to Do More 部分。

（二）教程的内容

1 《基础英语写作》(Foundation-Based English Writing)

本册教材从写作的角度出发，按照单词、句子、段落、篇章的顺序安排教学内容，旨在使学生在掌握最基本的语言知识后，学会如何去表达的英语写作能力。主要内容包括：

Unit 1	What Is a Word?
Unit 2	How to Choose Right Words?
Unit 3	What Is a Correct Sentence?
Unit 4	How to Use Effective Sentences?
Unit 5	What Is a Paragraph?
Unit 6	How to Write a Coherent Paragraph?
Unit 7	What Is an Essay?
Unit 8	How to Write a Clear Essay?

❷《实用英语写作》(Practical English Writing)

本册教材旨在提高学生实用英语写作基础知识，选题侧重于大学生在校期间常见的通知、个人书信、商业信件、留学申请、个人求职简历、读书报告、项目书等写作能力的掌握。主要内容包括：

Unit 1 How to Write a Note?
Unit 2 How to Write a Notice?
Unit 3 How to Write a Letter to a Friend?
Unit 4 How to Write a Business Letter?
Unit 5 How to Write an Application Letter for Studying Abroad?
Unit 6 How to Write a Reading Report?
Unit 7 How to Write a Resume?
Unit 8 How to Write a Proposal for a Research Program?

这两册书是写作教程的基础教材。因此，两册书的词汇起点基本按照教育部《普通高中英语课程标准》(2017 年版) 2 000 词设定。所有生词、短语、专有名词均按照在书中出现的顺序编排，标出词性，用汉语释义，帮助学生快速理解和掌握，排除阅读障碍。

本书配有教师用书，请登录中国人民大学出版社官方网站 (http://www.crup.com.cn) 搜索本书后下载使用，或联系 010-62515580，010-62512737，jialk@crup.com.cn, huangt@crup.com.cn 索取。

CONTENTS 目录

Unit 1

What Is a Word?

Highlights of this unit:

1. Defining a word
2. Classification of words
3. Syntactic functions of words
4. Use of words in context

Text A

Learning Mandarin, Whatever It Takes

A Today's *Wall Street Journal* offers a useful update to the annual "Americans are rushing to teach their kids Mandarin" story. The reporters have found several families that have gone to unusual lengths. One Californian lawyer took a year's leave of absence from work and moved the **clan** to Chengdu, for the sole purpose of immersion in the language. Another family moved to Singapore in 2007, again only so the kids could grow up speaking Mandarin. Other parents are not quite so committed, but nonetheless, families are enrolling their children in Mandarin-immersion programs that are springing up from California to Maine. They are hiring tutors, Skyping with teachers in Beijing and recruiting Chinese-speaking nannies. Some are stocking their playrooms with Disney videos in Mandarin — not to mention the iPhone apps aimed at making kids into Mandarin speakers.

B The article goes on that,

"Mandarin is notoriously difficult to learn. The language is tonal, and fluency requires mastering thousands of characters. Mandarin competence takes 2,200 class hours, with half of that time spent in a country where it's spoken, according to the U.S. State Department's Foreign Service Institute, whereas Spanish can be learned in 600 to 750 class hours."

C My upstairs neighbours' children have attended a Chinese-English bilingual school in New York for several years. It's the only public school of its kind in the city. Curious one day, I **plied** the younger one (eight years old) **with** a little quiz as we walked to the park with my son.

Me: "How do you say 'house'?"

Boy: "Uh, I forget."

Me: "How about 'car'?"

Boy: "Uh... hm..."

Me: "How about 'I am American'?"

Boy: "*Wo shi Zhongguo ren.*"

Me: "Hm, I'm pretty sure that means 'I am Chinese.' Isn't American *Meiguo ren*?"

Boy: "Oh, that's right!"

Me: "How about 'He is my friend.'?"

Boy: "Oh! *Ta shi wode pengyou.*"

Finally a perfect answer on the first go.

D This kid has been in this program since kindergarten. The Mandarin program is, strictly speaking, an after-school, voluntary one, but all kids go after school and study the language for 2.5 hours per day, I believe. At 180 school days a year, for just two years, he would have had roughly 900 hours of instruction and exposure, starting when he was quite small. (He may have had three years; I'm not sure.) Of course he's still quite small, and unlike State Department diplomats, doesn't have adult intellectual equipment to bring to bear. He does have a child's still-**plastic** brain, one of the reasons his accent was excellent. He's a bright kid. I can only take it that the State Department's statement is right: learning Mandarin is very hard for a native English-speaker, and true immersion is pretty important.

E I'm interested in the experience of those who have studied Chinese for a while. The Journal mentions both the **tones** and characters as difficulties, but I have a **hunch**: one problem is rather bigger than the other. Which is a tougher challenge: mastering and using the four tones (several each second) for accurate and fluent speech? Or learning the thousands of characters needed to read and write?

F I also know — because I've seen **calligraphy** homework around their apartment — that the kids spend significant time in reading and writing. Is this a good idea? Or would you focus on speech and use *pinyin* first with young children? The answers are important, as more and more Americans are going to be studying Mandarin in coming years, and getting the **pedagogy** right will be crucial.

New Words and Expressions

clan	*n.*	宗族
ply... with...		不停地提问
plastic	*adj.*	易塑造的
tone	*n.*	声调，字调
hunch	*n.*	直觉
calligraphy	*n.*	书法
pedagogy	*n.*	教学法

I Learn from the text

1. Read Text A and find which classes of words serve to convey the main idea of the passage.

____

____

2. Examine the first paragraph. Find the verbs first, then identify the different forms and explain the reasons for the change of form.

____

____

3. There are many "-ing" forms of verbs in the text. Can you tell the similarities and differences in terms of their use in the sentences?

____

____

Ⅱ Learn to know

1. Defining a word

Generally speaking, a word is defined as a minimal free form of a language that has a given sound, meaning and syntactic function. In other words, a word is characterized by the four aspects as shown in the box below.

Features of a word

- a unit of sound
- a unit of meaning
- a minimal free form of a language
- a form that can function alone in a sentence

2. Classification of words

There are a lot of ways to classify words in terms of writing, but syntactically, there are two types of words, namely, **Content Words** and **Function Words.**

Content Words are words that have referential meaning, usually including nouns, verbs, adjectives and adverbs. The examples of each class selected from the text are given in the table below:

Nouns	Verbs	Adjectives	Adverbs
language	learn	curious	nonetheless
lawyer	find	bilingual	always
update	offer	useful	quite
annual	teach	sole	so
kid	move	sure	pretty

There are a few other content words, for instance, negative words such as *no*, *not* and *never*; demonstrative pronouns including *this*, *that*, *these* and *those*; question words like *what*, *where*, *when*, *how* and *why*.

Function Words, also called structural words or grammatical words, are words that are used to connect meaning, or to establish the relationship between words, including auxiliary verbs, prepositions, articles, conjunctions and pronouns. The table below provides good examples:

Auxiliary Verbs	Prepositions	Articles	Conjunctions	Pronouns
do	in	a	and	I
have	between	an	so	you
be	to	the	but	we
would	for	–	or	they
could	about	–	yet	he

3. Syntactic functions of words

Words can be grammatically arranged to form sentences. A sentence is composed of different elements such as subject, predicate, object, object complement, adverbials, etc. These elements serve syntactic functions in the sentence. Let's analyze the following sentence taken from Text A to understand how words or phrases are used to perform syntactic functions.

Today's Wall Street Journal (noun phrase as subject)

offers a useful update to the annual

"Americans are rushing to teach their kids Mandarin" story.

(verb phrase as predicate)

A sentence can be divided into two parts: the subject (noun phrase) and the predicate (verb phrase). And the two parts can be subdivided into still smaller parts:

Today's Wall Street Journal (noun 's genitive + noun phrase)

offers a useful update (verb + noun phrase as direct object)

to the annual "Americans are rushing to teach their kids Mandarin" story

(prepositional phrase as preposition + indirect object)

The propositional phrase can be further broken down into:

to *the* *annual* *"Americans are rushing to teach their kids Mandarin"*

(prep.)(art.)(adjective as attribute) (sentence as attribute)

story

(noun as prepositional object)

The above analysis shows that words are arranged to form different phrases to realize different syntactic functions. The table below indicates how words and phrases are normally related to their syntactic functions:

Word/Word Phrases	Syntactic Functions
noun/noun phrase	subject, object, attribute
pronoun	subject, object
verb/verb phrase	predicate
adjective/adjective phrase	attribute, subject/object complement
adverb/adverb phrase	adverbial

Understanding how a sentence is formed in relation to the syntactic functions of words can help us to make correct sentences, but it is more important for us to learn how to use words in context.

4. Use of words in context

Verbs

It is important to fit the verb to the context. In Text A, the verbs conform to their subjects; to the tenses, moods and voices of their sentences; to the use of modals; etc.

Base	run	be(am, is, are)	have
Past	ran	-(was, were)	had
Past Participle	run	been	had
Present Participle	running	being	having
Gerund (noun)	running	being	having
Infinitive	to run	to be	to have

- **Choose the verb form that agrees with the subject in number and person.**

The Mandarin program ***is*** *strictly speaking an after-school, voluntary one, but all kids* ***go*** *after school and* ***study*** *the language for 2.5 hours per day, I* ***believe****.*

- **Choose the verb form that fits with the time frame.**

My upstairs neighbours' children ***have attended*** *a Chinese-English bilingual school in New York for several years.*

- **Use the base form of the verb following a modal verb.**

Another family moved to Singapore in 2007, again only so the kids could ***grow*** *up speaking Mandarin.*

- **Follow prepositions, articles, and possessive pronouns with the gerund form of verbs.**

The kids spend significant time in ***reading and writing***.

- **Some verbs often take an additional verb in the infinitive or gerund form as a complement.**

Verbs such as *decide*, *desire*, *hope*, *plan*, *wish*, *ask*, *choose*, *agree*, *seem*, etc., are usually followed by the infinitive form:

These may seem ***to be*** *quibbles.*

Verbs such as *enjoy*, *finish*, *practice*, *keep*, *mind*, *avoid*, *prevent*, etc., are followed by the gerund form:

He avoids ***talking*** to his parents all the time.

Nouns/Pronouns

Nouns and pronouns are closely connected with each other in English. Nouns refer to objects or persons and pronouns are used to substitute for nouns that appear before them in context. Nouns and pronouns must be in agreement with each other in number and person.

- **Plural nouns take a plural pronoun.**

Americans *are rushing to teach* ***their*** *kids Mandarin.*

The customers *finally got* ***their*** *compensation.*

- **Two nouns joined by *and* take a plural pronoun.**

The parent and the child *cleaned* ***their*** *house.*

The boys and the girl *handed in* ***their*** *homework.*

- **Nouns joined by *or* or *nor* take a pronoun agreeing with the noun that is near the verb.**

Neither the boys nor ***the girl*** *will bring* ***her*** *books.*

Either the girl or ***the boys*** *will bring* ***their*** *books.*

- **Collective nouns usually take a singular pronoun, but if they refer to individual persons, they take a plural pronoun.**

The class *is meeting in* ***its*** *scheduled room.*

The class *must hand in* ***their*** *homework on time.*

It is worth noticing that in some cases, such as the above sentence, no pronoun is needed. If the sentence is "The class must hand in homework on time," it would still be understood whose homework has to be handed in.

Adjectives

Adjectives also have inflections. There are three forms: positive, comparative, and superlative.

Generally speaking, the simplest form of the adjective is its positive form. When two objects or persons are being compared, the comparative form of the adjective is used. When three or more things are being compared, the superlative form of the adjective is used.

*The answers are **important**.*

*The Journal mentions both the tones and characters as difficulties, but I have a hunch one problem is rather **bigger** than the other.*

Adverbs

An adverb is a word that modifies a verb, an adjective, another adverb, or even a whole sentence. Adverbs often end in -ly, but some (such as *fast*) look exactly the same as their adjective counterparts.

*I'm **pretty** sure that means "I am Chinese."*

*I can **only** take it that the State Department's statement is right.*

Ⅲ Learn to do

1. Choose the more suitable word for each blank.

(1) One third of the population ________ (is, are) watching the show.

(2) Neither teachers nor the student ________ (know, knows) the answer.

(3) There ________ (is, are), however, numerous similarities between Ali and Laila.

(4) Neither the two cats nor the dog received ________ (its, theirs) food yesterday.

(5) None of the business owners felt that an increase in consumer

interest would threaten ________ (his, their) profitability.

(6) Some of the stamps belong to me, while the rest are ________ (his and hers, his and her).

(7) I suggest ________ (to do, doing) it in a different way.

(8) I can't imagine the girl ________ (speaking, speak) so rudely to you.

(9) Please remind me ________ (to leave, leaving) her this note.

(10) The job involves ________ (to travel, travelling) to London for three months.

2. Correct the error in each of the following sentences.

(1) While standing at the entrance of the restaurant, a waiter approached her.

____

____

____

(2) By advertising in the paper, Jim's house was quickly sold.

____

____

____

(3) Confused by his words, he explained it to me again.

____

____

____

(4) United as one, any difficulty can be overcome by them.

____

____

____

(5) To celebrate the festival, the room was decorated with flowers.

____

____

____

3. Use the proper form of the words in brackets to complete the summary of Text A.

The Wall Street Journal published a story about how some American families are so keen on ________ (teach) their children Mandarin that they have even moved to Chinese-speaking ________ (regional). One day, driven by ________ (curious), the author tested how ________ (good) his neighbours' boy knew the language. He estimated that the child had been learning Chinese for ________ (near) 900 hours. However, the boy's ability in Chinese was not encouraging, which led the author to reflect on how Chinese is taught and what the focus for children learning Chinese should be.

NOTES

Text B

The Biggest Vocabulary?

A Stephen Fry, whom I always enjoy, makes a claim:

[English] certainly has the largest vocabulary ... by a long, long, long, long way. Rather as China is to the rest of the world in population, English is in the population of its words.

B Is that true, a friend e-mails me to ask?

C There's a **longish** answer. For the summary version, skip to the end. For the really short version, though, the answer is "Sorry, Mr. Fry." English is certainly rich in vocabulary, but this claim is nearly always made by compareaholic lovers of English who don't really know how the many varieties of language beyond English work. It's not that another language has more words. The comparison simply can't be made in any agreed **apples-to-apples** way.

D The simplest problem is inflection. Do we count "run," "runs" and "ran" as separate? The next problem is multiple meanings. "Run" the verb and "run" the noun: one or two? What about "run" as in the long run of a play on Broadway? Different enough from a jog around the park for its own entry? Different enough from a run in cricket? Do we count compounds? Is "home run" one word or two? Are the names of new chemical compounds, which could be virtually infinite, words? What role does mere **orthographic** convention play? Is "home run" two words, but "homerun" (as it's often written) one? What sense does that make?

E These may seem to be **quibbles**, but discussing other languages, they become fundamental. Some languages **inflect** much more than English. The Spanish verb has dozens of forms — estoy, estás, está, "I am," "you are," "he is," and so on. Some languages inflect much less. (Chinese is famously ending-free.) So whether we count inflected forms will have a huge influence on final counts.

F Moreover, many languages habitually build long words from short ones. German is obvious. You've probably heard the Mark Twain gag: "Some German words are so long they have a perspective." You can make up crazy adjectives like my-recently-by-my-parents-thrown-out-of-the-window Play Station. Are compounds new words? Is the German *Unabhängigkeitserklärung*, "declaration of independence," one word? It's certainly written that way in German. Given the possibilities for compounds, German would quickly outstrip English, with new **legitimate** German "words," which Germans would accept without blinking, coined every day.

G Chinese people don't even deal primarily with our concept of "word" — their basic unit is the single one-syllable character, even though these are quite often combined into words. *Zhongguo* (中国) is "China." You can't just go looking for "Zhongguo" in the dictionary, though. You look up *zhong* (中 , middle), and the entry will tell you what " 中 " combines with to get different meanings. Learning what characters mean when used together is part of Chinese education. They are printed with no spaces. Does that mean *Zhongguo* isn't a word?

H We could go on in this **vein** for quite a while, but that will do for now. If I had to give a short answer to the question "Does English have the biggest vocabulary?", I'd say "Who cares?" English is a rich and beautiful language, not least because England has been conquered by Vikings and Normans, and has happily been open to foreign influence through its history. We know more of its wonderful rare words because English has been written for over a thousand years, and its many dialects are well described. I find it good enough for me. We shouldn't need it to have the biggest vocabulary — which can't be defined in any sensible way — to enjoy it.

New Words and Expressions

longish	*adj.*	稍长的，略长的
apples-to-apples		一一对等的
orthographic	*adj.*	正字法的
quibble	*n.*	小牢骚，小意见
inflect	*v.*	屈折变化，词尾变化
legitimate	*adj.*	合情合理的
vein	*n.*	方式，脉络

IV Learn to know more

Formation of English words

English has a large vocabulary. It is not necessary or possible to master all the words, but knowing some word-building strategies can help to significantly increase one's vocabulary and thus make one's descriptions more dramatic and vivid.

1. Derivation

Derivation is a way of forming words through adding an affix to a word stem. It can be divided into prefixation and suffixation. The former is a way of forming words by adding prefixes such as un-, multi-, in-, etc. For example, *unsuitable*, *multiple*, *infinite* (from Text B) are words formed through prefixation. The latter is a way of forming words by adding suffixes such as -ish, -ly, -ion, etc. *Longish*, *really*, *inflection* (from Text B) are such words formed through suffixation.

As derivation is useful in creating new words, it can also help improve the expressiveness of writing. Compare:

(1) a) *English is certainly rich in vocabulary, but this claim is nearly always made by **compareaholic** lovers of English who don't really know how the many varieties of language beyond English work.*

b) *English is certainly rich in vocabulary, but this claim is nearly always made by those lovers of English who always enjoy comparing English with other languages and don't really know how the many varieties of language beyond English work.*

Obviously, the use of the word ***compareaholic*** in (1) a) (from Text B) makes the expression much more concise than that in (1) b).The following are more examples of the same type:

(2) a) *This restaurant is* ***understaffed****.*

b) *This restaurant needs more staff.*

(3) a) *During graduation season, many fresh or soon-to-be graduates become* ***interviewaholics****.*

b) *During graduation season, many fresh or soon-to-be graduates become crazy about taking part in as many interviews as possible.*

2. Conversion

Conversion is a process that puts an existing word of one class into another class without changing its form. It is also called "zero derivation" and happens more frequently among nouns, verbs and adjectives.

Is that true, a friend ***e-mails*** *me to ask?*

E-mail is normally used as a noun. However, when used as a verb (as in Text B), the sentence is more concise, since "e-mails me to ask" is shorter than "sends me an e-mail to ask." Sometimes, conversions also occur when an auxiliary verb, a conjunction or an adverb is used as a verb or a noun. Some examples are given below:

To read English aloud is a ***must*** *for English majors.*

The world is full of excuses, so don't ***but*** *me so many* ***buts****.*

It is noticeable that verbs formed by conversions are plentiful and are often short, vivid and especially expressive when used in writing.

3. Compounding

Another common way to form words is compounding, which involves the combination of free morphemes. Compounds are written in different ways. As Text B shows, some can be written as a single word and some as two separate words, while some can be joined with a hyphen "-". *Homerun*, *home run* and *one-syllable* are examples.

An advantage of using compound nouns and adjectives in writing is that doing so can make for precise, vivid descriptions. Also, linking several words together with hyphens yields new compound adjectives that can make your writing not only more concise but also mildly humorous. The compound adjective in Paragraph F is a perfect example.

You can make up crazy adjectives like ***my-recently-by-my-parents-thrown-out-of-the-window*** *Play Station.*

The following are some additional examples:

(4) a) *The baby is seven months old, and she is at the stage when she enjoys putting things into her mouth.*

b) *The baby is seven months old, and she is at the* ***putting-things-into-her-mouth*** *stage.*

(5) a) *I really don't like the look on his face which suggests, "I told you so."*

b) *I really don't like the* ***I-told-you-so*** *look on his face.*

In each pair of sentences, the second one is more concise than the first one.

4. Clipping

Clipping is a process that shortens a polysyllabic word by deleting one or more syllables. Clipped words are initially used in spoken English or on informal occasions and should be avoided in writing. However, some clipped words now are widely accepted, and can be used even in formal writing. *Bus* (from omnibus), *fridge* (from refrigerator), *gym* (from gymnasium) and *vet* (from veterinarian or veteran) are good examples.

5. Blending

Blending is a process that creates new words by putting together non-morphemic parts of existing words. Examples include *smog* (smoke and fog) and *brunch* (a meal replacing breakfast and lunch). Some words are formed by a process that is partly blending and partly compounding. *Medicare* (medical plus care) and *guesstimate* (guess plus estimate) are formed in such a way.

V Learn to do more

1. Match the prefixes with their meanings.

(1) pre-	a. between/among
(2) fore-	b. before

(3) counter- c. across
(4) inter- d. against
(5) trans- e. first

2. In the passage, fill in each blank with the right form of the word in brackets, in each case using one of the prefixes immediately above. All five prefixes are used once each.

Commuting means to travel regularly back and forth. But it is ________ (dominate) related to travelling for work. A century ago, no one could have ________ (tell) how many commuters there would be today. Yet sometimes it seems all the advances in transport networks and developments in vehicles have been ________ (produce), for all we do is sit in traffic jams. It is kind of shameful that governments and construction companies have tried their best, only to find that the ________ (form) they had dreamed of has not happened. One reason is that the varied means of transport are ________ (depend), which means that a new system relies on other systems working alongside it.

3. Revise the following sentences with a compound to make them more concise.

E.g.: We had a meal in a farmhouse restaurant where for one price you could eat as much as you wanted.

Revised version: We had a meal in an "all-you-can-eat" farmhouse restaurant.

(1) Australia is a country which speaks English.

____

(2) His aunt looks good and works in an enterprise which is owned by the state.

____

(3) This is a plan that is well intentioned.

____

(4) This generally impatient attitude of hating to wait has infected every level of our lives.

____

(5) She says that she has outgrown the stage when she jumps on a chair at the sight of a mouse.

____

4. Guided writing.

Based on Text B, write a passage of about 200 words entitled "The Smaller the Vocabulary, the More Expressive the Chinese."

____

____

____

____

____

NOTES

Unit 2

How to Choose Right Words?

Highlights of this unit:

1. The stylistic meaning of words
2. General and specific words
3. Collocations
4. Connotation of words
5. Synonyms and antonyms

Text A

The Future of Higher Education

A No generation is more at ease with online, collaborative technologies than today's young people — "digital natives," who have grown up in an immersive computing environment. Where a notebook and pen may have formed the tool kit of prior generations, today's students come to class armed with smart phones, laptops and iPods.

B This era of pervasive technology has significant implications for higher education. Nearly two-thirds (63%) of survey respondents from the public and private sectors say that technological innovation will have a major impact on teaching methodologies over the next five years. "Technology allows students to become much more engaged in constructing their own knowledge, and cognitive studies show that ability is key to learning success," says New York City-based Queens College vice-president of institutional advancement, Susan Henderson.

C Online degree programmes and distance learning have gained a firm **foothold** in universities around the world. What was once considered a niche channel for the delivery of educational content has rapidly become mainstream, creating wider access to education, new markets for content and expanded **revenue** opportunities for academic institutions. Sixty percent of those polled say that the technological change occurring in our **midst** will alter the perception of the college campus from a one-dimensional (physical) concept to a multi-dimensional (physical and online) one. "Law school students enrolled in hybrid programmes that integrate distance and in-class education outperform those who study exclusively in one environment," says Tom Delaney, associate dean and CIO of the New York University (NYU) School of Law, of the results of a recent limited trial at his school.

D New technologies are also affecting other areas of campus administration. Social-networking tools are helping to build connections with alumni and support career service activities. E-marketing campaigns expand the reach and success of recruiting and fundraising efforts, and drive down the cost of direct-mail campaigns. And automated, self-service programmes reduce administrative requirements, streamline course registration and enhance academic life.

E Although university participants view these changes as having a largely positive impact, many institutions struggle with the twin challenges of rising information technology (IT) costs and the need to avoid technological obsolescence. In addition, insufficient resources, a lack of adequate instructional design staff and other technological support issues can also impede the adoption of new technologies. Despite these challenges, most believe that technology will become ever more interwoven into the fabric of academic life.

New Words and Expressions

foothold	*n.*	立足点
revenue	*n.*	财政收入
midst	*n.*	中间
alumni	*n.*	（统称）校友
streamline	*v.*	使……效率更高
obsolescence	*n.*	过时；陈旧

I Learn from the text

1. Compare the two sentences in each pair and tell the differences between them.

(1) a. Sixty percent of those polled say that the technological change occurring in our midst will alter the perception of the college campus from a one-dimensional (physical) concept to a multi-dimensional (physical and online) one. (from Paragraph C)

b. Sixty percent of those polled say that the technological change occurring among us will change the image of the college campus from a one-dimensional (physical) concept to a multi-dimensional (physical and online) one.

(2) a. Nearly two-thirds (63%) of survey respondents from the public and private sectors say that technological innovation will have a major impact on teaching methodologies over the next five years. (from Paragraph B)

b. A lot of the respondents say that technological innovation will have a major impact on teaching methodologies over the coming years.

2. Identify as many word collocations as possible in the text.

Ⅱ Learn to know

1. The stylistic meaning of words

English is rich in vocabulary; therefore, word choice can make an enormous difference in the quality of writing. From a stylistic point of view, English words can be classified into three types: common, formal and colloquial.

Common (standard) words are those ordinary and familiar words people use every day, and they appear in all kinds of writing. The majority of Text A consists of common words — ***no, generation, more, ease, online, technology*** and ***young***, to name just a few.

Formal words are used by people in special professions, or on special occasions, or for special purposes. Many such words are of Greek or Latin origin. They usually appear in formal writing, such as academic or theoretical works, political and legal documents, and formal lectures and addresses. As you read Text A, you may spot a lot of formal words such as ***collaborative, immersive, era, pervasive, engaged, foothold, midst, perception, impede,*** and ***obsolescence.***

Colloquial words are usually used in informal or familiar conversations. They rarely appear in formal writing, and in literary works their main use is to record people's thoughts and dialogue. For example, *guts*, *guy* and *bro* are words of this type.

Text A is extracted from an Economist Intelligence Unit white paper. It is an academic report on how technology will shape learning in the future. Academic writing is usually considered formal. The author in this case writes in a formal style with no colloquial language. The following pair of sentences illustrates how word selection goes in line with the overall style and purpose of writing in Text A:

a) "Sixty percent of those polled say that the technological change occurring in our **midst** will **alter** the **perception** of the college campus from a one-dimensional (physical) concept to a multi-dimensional (physical and online) one." (from Paragraph C)

b) "Sixty percent of those polled say that the technological change occurring **among** us will **change** the **image** of the college campus from a one-dimensional (physical) concept to a multi-dimensional (physical and online) one."

The two sentences are basically the same in structure and meaning, but they are distinctive in the stylistic choice of words. The first sentence is relatively formal due to the use of such words as ***midst, alter*** and ***perception***, being consistent with the formality of Text A. In contrast, the second sentence is less formal. Typical examples of the above-mentioned three types of words are given in the table.

Types	Examples			
formal	displease	adult male	fortitude	infant
common	bother	man	courage	baby
colloquial	hassle	guy	guts	kid

Another thing one should bear in mind is that the formality of words is a matter of degree. One word may be slightly more formal than another. For instance, ***difficult*** may be more formal than ***hard*** which is more formal than ***tricky***. Enhancing one's stylistic awareness enables one to write in a more appropriate way.

2. General and specific words

There is also a distinction between general and specific words. Some words are more general or more specific in meaning than others. For example, *language* is a general word compared with *English*, *Spanish*, *Russian* and *Chinese* as specific words. *Gender* is a general word, while *feminine* and *masculine* are specific words. Both general and specific words are valuable in writing. General words are often used to express general ideas, but when describing or explaining things in detail, the use of more specific words can be supporting, vivid and exact. Take Paragraph D in Text A as an example. In this paragraph, the general word ***new technology*** is presented in the beginning sentence to show the general idea. Then it is supported by the use of specific words — such as ***social-networking tools***, ***e-marketing***, ***automated***, ***self-service programme*** — as concrete examples.

Here are typical examples of general and specific words in contrast.

General	Specific
laugh	smile, giggle
athlete	basketball player, football player
student	freshmen, sophomore
flower	rose, lily
scientist	chemist, physicist

Note that a good piece of writing often uses both general and specific words to achieve the desired effect.

3. Collocations

Collocations are sequences of words or terms that co-occur more often than would be expected by chance. They are expressions habitually used by native speakers. In Text A, expressions like ***at ease with, arm with, have an impact on, be engaged in, gain a foot hold, access to, struggle with, access to, in our midst, engaged in*** are all collocations. Some other typical collocations are shown in the table below.

Verb + Noun	Adjective/Noun + Noun	Noun/Adjective + Preposition
acquire knowledge	thick soup	attitude to/toward
get a job	strong tea	interested in
achieve success	vice president	dependent on
gain reputation	deputy manager	independent of
attain one's ends	counterfeit money	tired of
reach a conclusion	artificial flowers	lack of

Note that there are varieties of collocations in English which are actually fixed expressions. For example, in Text A the titles of the two quoted experts are *vice-president* and *associate dean*, though in Chinese, we use the same adjective to describe the position, *fuzongtong* (副总统) *and fuyuanzhang* (副院长). Again, in Chinese we say *daxue* (大雪), but in English we often say "heavy snow" instead of "big snow." Also in English, "make a big mistake" or "make a great mistake" is a collocation but not "make a large mistake." We have to learn them by heart.

Ⅲ Learn to do

I. Replace the underlined formal words in each sentence with more common ones.

(1) The work was arduous.

(2) Before he died, he had consumed a large quantity of alcohol.

(3) The students all endeavor to finish the job by next week.

(4) The Romans were the first to utilized concrete as a building material.
(5) I am unable to find her residence because of the poor weather.
(6) A good use of words does not mean the employment of big words.
(7) The meeting is scheduled to commence at noon.
(8) Your contract of employment terminates in December.
(9) It was a very patent lie.
(10) The famous singer dwells in the small town during most of the year.

2. Rewrite the following passage by using more specific words.

John, the athlete, had a great day. For starters, he did well in the race. In addition, it was his birthday. His family prepared a party for him. He received some great presents from his friends. They had a great time together. The icing on the cake was that the city council granted him a title on this special occasion. He said he would never forget this day.

____

____

____

____

____

3. Identify the wrong collocation and provide a correct one.

(1) You can **learn knowledge** from reading.

____

(2) I **ate breakfast** with my best friend today.

____

(3) After three months' hard work, she **made large progress** in English.

____

(4) It is good for one's health to **drink soup** every day.

____

(5) His girlfriend **spreads perfume** every day.

____

(6) Whatever reasons she may give, I will not **change my idea**.

____

(7) We must **try all our efforts** to solve the problem.

____

(8) Because of the **crowded traffic**, it took me forever to get home.

____

(9) Although it is not easy to learn English well, I will never **lose my heart**.

____

(10) Addiction to the Internet can **have some unhealthy habits**.

____

NOTES

Text B

The Minimalist Classroom

A The classroom is a teacher's arena; it projects powerful **subliminal** messages to the group of young people in it. Its make-up will, in part, influence their responses to our teaching and their motivation in our subjects.

B One of the issues in the modern classroom is the **ubiquity** of stuff that dominates every spare inch. Resources, workbooks, equipment and increasingly elaborate visual displays all **vie** for limited space. Inevitably, this results in an environment that is distracting and loud, and that can easily become disorganised — not the best mix when trying to inspire the calm and focus of 30 boisterous adolescents.

C There is also the impact of all this additional stuff on our own emotions in the classroom: Is it feeding any anxious thoughts we might have about our jobs? Would a more streamlined approach help us to feel less stressed, and aid our clarity of thought in the environment in which we spend an **inordinate** amount of our time?

D We may believe that our classrooms are organised and project clarity, but are we secretly teacher magpies? Take 15 minutes to look at your room from a renewed perspective and think: What image am I projecting? How much of the environment is helpful to enable young people to learn and concentrate?

E We all know the wonderful lightness of spirit we experience after doing a spring clean. This image of renewal and **serenity** should be kept in mind to encourage a minimalist review of your classroom. Be ruthless: What isn't having a transferable impact on students' ability to learn?

F The best place to start is to tackle the **clutter**: What is lurking in corners of the room that can be removed? When was the last time it was used? What are the pieces of paper that can be scanned and saved to that wonderful de-cluttering enabler: the trusty memory stick? Once you have adopted this purging mindset, apply it to the equipment and to the dusty posters: Are they enabling learning, or a distraction?

G Some of us don't have the pleasure of ownership of our own rooms. Here, it is about travelling light with the bare essentials and seeking to encourage colleagues to see the value of adopting the minimalist attitude. Once we model the way and highlight the impact on our students, our colleagues will embrace the less-is-more approach.

New Words and Expressions

subliminal	*adj.*	下意识的
ubiquity	*n.*	普遍
vie	*v.*	竞争
inordinate	*adj.*	过度的；过分的
serenity	*n.*	宁静
clutter	*n.*	杂乱

Ⅳ Learn to know more

1. Connotation of words

Connotation refers to the implied meaning or association of a word or phrase apart from the thing it explicitly identifies. Careful writers choose words both for what they mean (that is, their denotations) and for what they suggest (their emotional associations or connotations). For instance, the nouns *group*, *clique*, and *club* all have basically the same denotative meaning: a set of more than one person. However, each of these words has a different connotative meaning. The following table illustrates the differences:

club	group	clique
positive connotation	neutral connotation	negative connotation
refers to a collection of people that voluntarily come together for a shared passion or purpose.	bears no positive or negative feelings, simply refers to a bunch of people.	usually used in circumstances where the group is known for excluding others.

The example (from Text B) "*The classroom is a teacher's arena; it projects powerful subliminal messages to the group of young people in it.*" shows that the use of *group* with neutral connotation fits in best with what the author really means. More examples are shown in the table below.

Positive Connotation	Neutral Connotation	Negative Connotation
employ	use	exploit
club	group	clique
steadfast	tenacious	stubborn
sated	filled	crammed
courageous	confident	conceited
unique	different	peculiar
frugal, thrifty	money-saving, economical	stingy, tight-fisted
vintage	old	decrepit
elated	happy	manic

2. Synonyms and antonyms

Synonyms are words having the same or similar meanings. Antonyms are words that have the opposite meaning to one another.

In writing, one may deliberately employ synonyms and antonyms for the sake of variety, emphasis, and contrast. For example, in Text B, the author uses synonyms such as ***anxious*** and ***stressed***, ***aid*** and ***help***, ***influence*** and ***impact***, ***adolescence*** and ***young people*** to add variety to the writing. Antonymous expressions such as ***organised*** and ***disorganised***, ***anxious thoughts*** and ***clarity of thought*** are used for the sake of contrast.

One should be aware that words may only be roughly or approximately synonymous. It is difficult to find two words that share the exact same meaning and use. Synonyms can be different in connotation, style, degree of emphasis, emotional coloring, tone, and collocation. The following sentences may help illustrate how to use synonyms and antonyms appropriately.

(1) a. He promised to finish his homework on Saturday, but he ***neglected*** it and handed it in on Sunday.

b. His teacher asked him to finish his homework on Saturday, but he ***ignored*** it and decided to go swimming instead.

(2) a. We'd better make good use of this opportunity to ***acquire*** new skills.

b. We'd better make good use of this opportunity to ***obtain*** some new information.

(3) Inevitably, this results in an environment that is ***distracting*** and ***loud***, and that can easily become ***disorganized*** — not the best mix when trying to inspire the *calm* and *focus* of 30 **boisterous** adolescents.

(4) People used to believe that the world's supply of energy would ***last*** forever, but now it seems that our supplies of coal and oil are about to ***run out***.

As the above examples suggest, it is important to study synonyms and understand their nuances, so that one can appropriately apply them in writing. It is a good habit to have a dictionary handy when we write.

V Learn to do more

I. Choose the word whose connotation best matches the sentence.

(1) The girl ________ (closed, slammed) the door behind her, threw her bag on the floor and slumped into a wooden chair, where she poured herself a much-needed glass of wine.

(2) The French are ________ (noted, notorious) for their fine food.

(3) The mother tenderly ________ (smiled, smirked) at her newborn baby through the hospital nursery window.

(4) The local newspaper's front-page story reported that £10,000 was ________ (taken, stolen) from the city's largest bank during the night.

(5) One of them is that happy moment at the soda fountain... with a tinkling glass of ________ (freezing, ice-cold) Coca-Cola.

2. Write short passages according to the guidelines given.

A. Douglas was careful with his money. He kept his money in a safe place and bought only necessities. More importantly, he never borrowed or lent money.

(1) Describe your impression of Douglas's thrift.

____

____

____

(2) Make fun of Douglas or criticize him for being such a tightwad.

____

____

____

B. You see a person of average weight, with brown hair and a small nose, wearing casual clothes.

(1) Tell a friend, in an informal way, what the person looked like and your opinion of this person in negative tone.

____

____

____

(2) In a more formal way, describe the person's appearance and comment on the person's possible habits and attitudes in positive tone.

____

____

____

3. **Write a paragraph that describes your ideal classroom. Pay special attention to your choice of words.**

NOTES

Unit 3

What Is a Correct Sentence?

Highlights of this unit:

1. Defining a correct sentence
2. Identifying basic sentence patterns
3. Expanding basic sentence patterns

Text A

A Winter's Tale

Vance and Marcia Fry

On a cold winter weekend, a young couple is warmed by the kindness of strangers.

A We could die out here. Sitting in our **stalled** car, 240 km from home, we couldn't help but worry. It was around 10 p.m. on a bitterly cold, mid-winter night. We didn't have a phone, and we didn't know how far away the nearest town was. Worst of all, nobody knew where we were.

B Well, almost nobody. One man had stopped to help us — he said he'd call a tow truck. But 45 minutes later, we found our toes getting numb, and the truck was nowhere in sight. Sitting in our freezing car, we never could have guessed that the weekend would have a joyful ending.

C After another 15 minutes, the tow truck finally arrived. We gratefully crawled into the truck's heat-filled cab. Charging us $50 for the 4-minute ride, the driver took us to a hotel in the tiny town of Rum River, Minnesota. We were far from home and from our original destination — a church gathering in northern Minnesota.

D As **newlyweds**, we didn't have much money, so we asked for an inexpensive room. The manager said, "That'll be $45. But I'll only charge you $5 more for the honeymoon suite." We accepted his offer. Complete with a king-size bed, big screen TV and heart-shaped **Jacuzzi**, the room almost made up for getting **stranded**.

The Kindness of Strangers

E The next morning, we picked up the phone to try to find a way to get our car home. The local garages were closed for the weekend. We managed to contact a **mechanic** who was working in a town nearby. He promised to take a look at our car — if we could get it to him. Strangely, our car started fine. But would we make it to the mechanic?

F Five minutes down the highway, our car stalled again. We knocked on the doors of nearby houses, looking for help. At the third house, a **gruff**-looking man opened the door and let us use his phone.

G He introduced himself as Bill. It became clear that under his gruff exterior was a kind heart. His friend owned a tow truck and could help us that afternoon. Bill and his wife Dawn urged us to make ourselves at home. Dawn fixed us lunch and chatted with us as if we were old friends, not strangers she'd just met.

H It was easy to believe we were friends. Bill and Dawn had so much in common with us. Surprisingly, we knew many of the same places and people. Our churches were even related. So far from home, meeting the couple seemed like more than just a **coincidence**.

The Trip Home

I When the tow truck arrived, Dawn handed us a $150 check. "Not much," she said, "but just a little something to help you get home." We tried to turn down the money, but Dawn insisted. We'd been a **blessing** to her, she said. She'd been under the weather all week and had needed some company. For Dawn as well as for us, our broken-down car had turned out to be **a blessing in disguise**.

J Rick, the tow truck driver, was surprised that we'd only owned our car for 10 days. He said we should take the car back to the **dealership** where we'd bought it.

K During the trip back to the dealership, we found out that we'd gone to college with Rick's daughter and had several mutual friends. The two-hour drive passed quickly. After dropping the car off at the dealership, Rick took us to the nearby college where we'd studied. A friend or family member could take us the extra 20 minutes back to our home.

L A two-hour trip in a tow truck should have cost nearly $200. But Rick's price? "Oh just give me $45 for fuel," he said. We were thankful, but hardly surprised. Rick's gift was the perfect ending to a weekend full of blessings provided through the generosity of strangers.

New Words and Expressions

stall	*v.*	（车辆或发动机）熄火，抛锚
newlyweds	*n.*	新婚夫妇
Jacuzzi	*n.*	按摩浴缸
stranded	*adj.*	陷于困境的
mechanic	*n.*	技工，机修工
gruff	*adj.*	（指人的声音或行为）生硬的；粗野的，粗暴的
coincidence	*n.*	巧合（的事）
blessing	*n.*	祝福
a blessing in disguise		初看似乎不幸，然而过后看来却是幸运的事；祸中福
dealership	*n.*	代理商，经销商

I Learn from the text

1. Read the following sentences and point out what common feature in structure they have.

(1) We could die out here.

____

(2) We were far from home.

____

(3) His friend owned a tow truck.

____

(4) You can just give me $45.

____

(5) We found our toes getting numb.

____

2. Identify the components of each sentence's structure.

(1) The two-hour drive passed quickly.

____

(2) Nobody knew where we were.

____

(3) Dawn fixed us lunch.

(4) He introduced himself as Bill.

(5) We were thankful, but hardly surprised.

3. Identify the independent and dependent clauses or subordinating phrases of the following sentences.

(1) We didn't have a phone, and we didn't know how far away the nearest town was.

(2) As newlyweds, we didn't have much money, so we asked for an inexpensive room.

(3) Complete with a king-size bed, big screen TV and heart-shaped Jacuzzi, the room almost made up for getting stranded.

(4) We managed to contact a mechanic who was working in a town nearby.

(5) We knocked on the doors of nearby houses, looking for help.

II Learn to know

1. Defining a correct sentence

A sentence is a set of words that is complete in itself, typically containing a subject and a predicate, conveying a statement, question, exclamation, or command, and consisting of a main clause and sometimes one or more subordinate clauses. A correct sentence must be complete in form and logical in meaning. The following examples fail to meet the requirements of a correct sentence.

* The dog was born on Christmas Eve in 2002

* the poor dog could not walk and even his mother did not want him.

* Jude met the dog and wanted to take care.

* The dog was named "Faith," so he grew stronger and stronger.

What is wrong with each example? Looking carefully, we find that the period in the first sentence is missing; the second one does not begin with a capital letter; the third one is not complete in meaning; and the last one contains two ideas which are not logically related.

Basic knowledge of a correct sentence

It is complete in structure.
It begins with a capital letter.
It ends with a period (.), or a question mark (?), or an exclamation mark (!).
It contains a single complete idea, the elements of which are logically related.

2. Identifying basic sentence patterns

Sentences are structural units for writing. There may seem to be countless diverse sentence patterns in English, but, in fact, there are only five basic sentence patterns from which all sentences are derived.

SV: Subject + V (intransitive verb as predicate)
SVC: Subject + V (linking verb) + Subject Complement
SVO: Subject + V (transitive verb) + Object
SVOO: Subject + V (transitive verb) + Indirect Object + Direct Object
SVOC: Subject + V (transitive verb) + Object + Object Complement

A simple sentence at least contains one subject and one verb. The test for a correct sentence is to ask a question: **Who** or **what** is doing **what action**? The word or phrase that addresses the **who-or-what** question is the **subject**. The word or phrase that addresses the **what-action** question is the **verb**. So "S+V" is the core in any sentence pattern.

- **SV**

This pattern, with an intransitive verb as the predicate, can express a complete idea without taking an object.

S	Vi
The two-hour drive	passed quickly.
A light heart	lives long.
Great minds	think alike.

- **SVC**

This pattern has a linking verb — such as *be*, *get*, *seem*, *grow*, etc. — as its predicate, followed by the subject complement that shows the subject's features, qualities or state.

S	V(linking verb)	C
Our toes	were getting	numb.
They	are	married.
Virtue	never grows	old.

- **SVO**

In this pattern, the predicate is a transitive verb, which is followed by an object.

S	Vt	O
His friend	owned	a tow truck.
Good fences	make	good neighbors.
Good manners	define	the gentleman.

- **SVOO**

In this pattern, the predicate is a transitive verb that can take two objects: the indirect object and the direct object. Usually the indirect object is someone, and the direct object is something.

S	Vt	O_1	O_2
Dawn	handed	us	a $150 check.
Mother	bought	me	a new dress.
Mr. Lee	offers	Peter	a great chance.

Note that if the indirect object is moved after the direct object, a preposition is needed between the two objects.

Dawn handed a $150 check to us.
Mother bought a new dress for me.
Mr. Lee offers a great chance to Peter.

- SVOC

The predicate in this pattern is also a transitive verb that can take a complex object — namely, an object and its complement. The complement, used to complete the meaning of the object, can be a noun, an adjective, an adverb, or an infinitive, -ing or -ed form.

S	V	O	C
They	have made	me	the chairman.
Early to bed and early to rise,	makes	a man	healthy, wealthy and wise.
An apple a day	keeps	the doctor	away.
The robber	forced	us	to leave the office.
I	heard	Jean	singing an old song.
We	saw	the road	covered with snow.

3. Expanding basic sentence patterns

Basic sentence patterns can be combined to form compound sentences, complex sentences, and compound-complex sentences.

- **Compound sentences**

A compound sentence expresses two or more equally important ideas which are connected by coordinating conjunctions or conjunctive adverbs. The following table shows what the commonly used coordinating conjunctions are and how they are used to connect compound sentences.

Our toes were getting numb,	***and***	the truck was nowhere in sight.
One can't help many,	***but***	many can help one.
Someone should do something,	***or***	something bad will happen.
Happiness is a point of view,	***so***	in order to feel better, change your perspective.
He cannot rely on anyone now,	***nor***	does he expect to rely on anyone in the future.
I don't eat much,	***yet***	I have to wear XL.
He must be out,	***for***	there is no light in the room.

It should be pointed out that a comma often (but not always) comes before the conjunction, signaling that another important idea follows. Besides the coordinating conjunctions shown in the table, there are common correlative conjunctions, such as *either...or...*, *not only... but also...*, and so on.

The conjunctive adverbs often used to connect compound sentences are *therefore*, *however*, *nonetheless*, *hence*, *otherwise*, *besides*, *moreover*, etc. Unlike conjunctions, however, when a conjunctive adverb is used, a **semicolon,** instead of a **comma,** usually ends the first main clause. Take a look at the examples in the following table:

Some people have had bad experiences with strangers;	***therefore***, *they don't trust them.*
He has been cheated and has lost a lot of money;	***however***, he still has faith in others.
She was very tired;	***nonetheless***, she kept on working.
The trade imbalance is likely to occur again;	***hence*** a new set of policies are required.
We must go early;	***otherwise***, we may not get a seat.
She does all the housework every day;	***besides***, she has to send the kids to school.
The rich man built a Hope School in the countryside;	***moreover***, he donated a thousand books to the village library.

Note that, in some cases, the semicolon can be omitted (and often replaced by a comma) if a coordinating conjunction such as "and" is added before the conjunctive adverb. For example, "I don't really want to go, and besides, it's too late now."

- **Complex sentences**

A complex sentence contains a main clause and one or more subordinate clauses, which are introduced by subordinating conjunctions (*that*, *if*, *whether*, *because*, etc.) or relative pronouns (*who*, *whom*, *whoever*, *which*, *that*, *whichever*, *whatever*, etc.) or conjunctive adverbs (*when*, *where*, *why*, *how*, etc.), as shown in the table below.

Subject clause	**That** the planets are moving is not beyond dispute. **How** she wrote her first book is a story itself.
Object clause	Everything depends on **whether** we have enough time. He made it clear **that** he objected to the plan.

Predicative clause	The truth is **that** not all love stories have a happy ending. My question is **where** I can get my car repaired.
Appositive clause	The readers were surprised at the fact **that** he traveled across the U.S. relying on the kindness of strangers. Evidence came up **that** specific speech sounds are recognized by babies as young as six months old.
Relative clause	We managed to contact a mechanic **who** was working in a town nearby. This is the house **in which** I have lived for ten years.
Adverbial clause	He promised to take a look at our car — **if** we could get it to him. **When** the tow truck arrived, Dawn handed us a $150 check.

- **Compound-complex sentences**

A compound-complex sentence is a sentence made up of two independent clauses and at least one dependent clause. For example: "We didn't have a phone, and we didn't know how far away the nearest town was." This sentence contains two independent clauses: "We didn't have a phone" and "we didn't know how far away the nearest town was," which includes a dependent clause, "how far away the nearest town was."

In this example, there are two independent clauses connected by "and." The second independent clause is a complex sentence that contains an object clause. So the whole sentence is classified as a compound-complex sentence.

Ⅲ Learn to do

1. Keeping in mind what makes a correct sentence, correct the errors in the following sentences.

(1) Although failed, it was worth doing.

____

____

(2) There were fifty students attended the lecture.

____

____

(3) Due to unfavorable conditions, the sports meet has been canceled, we are very disappointed.

(4) By attending recreational activities on campus can cultivate students' ability.

(5) If a man works without taking a break, which could result in serious harm to his body.

2. Answer the following questions, using as many compound and complex sentences as possible, and label the sentence types you use.

(1) Who is one of your heroes?

(2) What is the main reason that you consider this person a hero?

(3) What is his or her typical character?

(4) Can you tell something to illustrate your hero's character?

(5) How does this person influence the way you live?

3. Combine the sentences with appropriate connective words.

(1) I met the local people.
I was grateful to them for their rides, their food, their shelter, and their gifts.

(2) His wife, Carol, a seventh-grade science teacher, was cooking a pot roast.
We walked into the kitchen.

(3) This woman was telling me something.
She'd rather risk her life than feel bad about passing a stranger on the side of the road.

(4) It is not death that a man should fear.
He should fear never live truly.

(5) He went to the department store.
He returned with a little box.
The box contained his special gift to his wife.

Text B

Giving Life Meaning

James Rick

A Have you thought about what you want people to say about you after you're gone? Can you hear the voices saying, "He was a great man." or "She really will be missed."? What else do they say?

B One of the strangest phenomena of life is to engage in work that will last long after death. Isn't that a lot like investing all your money so that future generations can bear interest on it? Perhaps, yet if you look deep in your own heart, you'll find something drives you to make this kind of contribution — something drives every human being to find a purpose that lives on after death.

C Do you hope to **memorialize** your name? Have a name that is whispered with **reverent** awe? Do you hope to have your face carved upon 50 feet of **granite** rock? Is the answer really that simple? Is the purpose of a lifetime contribution an ego-driven desire for a **mortal** being to have an immortal name — or is it something more?

D A child alive today will die tomorrow. A baby that had the potential to be the next Einstein will die from **complications** at birth. The circumstances of life are not set in stone. We are not all meant to live life through to old age. We've grown to perceive life as a full cycle with a certain number of years in between. If all of those years aren't lived out, it's a tragedy. A tragedy because a human's potential was never realized. A tragedy because a spark was **snuffed out** before it ever became a flame.

E **By virtue of** inhabiting a body we accept these risks. We expose our mortal flesh to the laws of the physical environment around us. The **trade off** isn't so bad when you think about it. The problem comes when we construct mortal fantasies of what life should be like. When life doesn't **conform to** our fantasy, we grow upset, frustrated, or depressed.

F We are alive; let us live. We have the ability to experience; let us experience. We have the ability to learn; let us learn. The meaning of life can be grasped in a moment. A moment so brief it often **evades** our perception.

G What meaning stands behind the dramatic unfolding of life? What single truth can we grasp and hang onto for dear life when all other truths around us seem to fade with time?

H These moments are strung together in a series we call events. These events are strung together in a series we call life. When we seize the moment and bend it according to our will, a will driven by the spirit deep inside us, then we have discovered the meaning of life, a meaning for us that shall go on long after we depart this Earth.

New Words and Expressions

memorialize	*v.*	纪念
reverent	*adj.*	恭敬的
granite	*n.*	花岗岩
mortal	*adj.*	凡人的，必有一死的
complication	*n.*	并发症
snuff out		掐灭，扼杀
by virtue of		由于，凭借
trade off		权衡，交易
conform to		符合，遵照
evade	*v.*	逃避

IV Learn to know more

1. The use of four kinds of sentences in writing

One of the striking features of Text B is the use of interrogative sentences, which, by definition, ask questions. Besides asking questions, they may function to introduce, to emphasize, to enlighten, etc. If we classify sentences in terms of function, there are four kinds: declarative, interrogative, imperative, and exclamatory.

A declarative sentence makes a statement. It is the most common sentence type. For example: "We expose our mortal flesh to the laws of the physical environment around us."

An interrogative sentence asks a question. This may be a *yes–no* question or a *wh*-question. In writing, a question can be asked to draw the readers' attention and arouse their interest. For example, in Text B many interrogative sentences are well used to pave a path for the readers to go deeper into the theme of the text.

The question, which is often asked to make a point rather than to require an answer, is called a rhetorical question. For example:

Isn't that a lot like investing all your money so that future generations can bear interest on it? (That is a lot like investing all your money...)

Is the answer really that simple? (The answer is not really that simple.)

How can the blind belief of sentimentality be sensible or rewarding? (The blind belief of sentimentality isn't sensible or rewarding.)

Haven't multitudes perished spiritually for the lack of another's belief in them? (Multitudes have perished spiritually for the lack of another's belief in them.)

Can anyone doubt there are some dark corners which do not react to sweetness and light? (Surely there are some dark corners which do not react to sweetness and light.)

An imperative sentence makes a command or a request. In writing, imperative sentences are often used when you give instructions or call for action. For example:

We are alive; *let us live*. We have the ability to experience; *let us experience*. We have the ability to learn; *let us learn*.

After separating them from the yolks, beat the whites until they are light and fluffy.

Let's take action now to protect our environment.

An exclamatory sentence expresses strong emotions, or involuntary reactions. It can be manifested as a one- or two-word interjection, or as a major sentence. For example:

Ouch!

What an amazing world it would be if everyone had faith in others!

How disappointing (it is) to be misunderstood when trying to help a stranger!

2. The use of apposition in writing

Apposition is a grammatical **construction in which two elements** (normally noun phrases) are placed side by side, with one element serving to identify the other in a different way. The two elements are said to be "in apposition." In writing, apposition is often used to define, to explain, to clarify, or to provide context or additional strength to the thing being described. For example: "When we seize the moment and bend it according to our will, a will driven by the spirit deep inside us, then we have discovered the meaning of life, a meaning for us that shall go on long after we depart this Earth." This sentence uses apposition to explain "our will" and "the meaning of life."

3. The use of conditional clauses in writing

Conditional clauses, describing real or hypothetical situations, are often used to illustrate or clarify the writer's opinion or stance. For example:

If all of those years aren't lived out, it's a tragedy. (real condition)

Perhaps, yet if you look deep in your own heart, you'll find something drives you to make this kind of contribution — something drives every human being to find a purpose that lives on after death. (real condition)

If I were rich, I would buy a boat.(unreal condition)

If the weather had been nice last weekend, we would have barbecued. (unreal condition)

V Learn to do more

1. Write a paragraph according to the situation provided, using proper conditional clauses.

Situation 1: Suppose a good friend asks you to help him to cheat on an exam. What would you do? Help him break the rules or refuse to help him and risk losing his friendship?

Situation 2: Suppose you are in a hurry to get to school, and you see a purse by the roadside. What would you do? Try to find the owner or ignore it in order not to be late for school?

Situation 3: Suppose your roommate is smoking in your dorm room and cigarette smoke irritates your eyes and throat. Would you ask him to stop, or would you leave the room without interrupting him?

Situation 4: Jim is a policeman. He one day runs into Bob, a childhood friend he has not seen for many years. He discovers Bob is a wanted criminal. What would you do if you were Jim: arrest Bob or ignore his criminality and renew your friendship? Justify your choice.

____

____

____

____

____

Situation 5: Returning home from work one night, Jane notices someone breaking into her neighbor's house. If you were Jane, what would you do?

____

____

____

____

____

2. In the following, five students are discussing whether artificial intelligence will make humans lazy thinkers. Help them complete the opinions, using indicated sentence types.

Student 1: Artificial intelligence will make our brains more creative rather than lazier. Thanks to intelligent machines, ______________________________ (simple sentence) In addition, with intelligent machines, ______________________________ (simple sentence) Therefore, ______________________________ (any sentence type)

Student 2: I disagree that artificial intelligence will make our brains lazy, ______________________________ (complex sentence) With the help of intelligent machines, ______________________________ (simple sentence)

Student 3: Artificial intelligence has wide application in many aspects of life. Not only ________ but also ________ (compound sentence) Rarely is a frog being boiled in warm water likely to realize that he is in danger. Fortunately, ________ (any sentence type) This is the embodiment of human wisdom.

Student 4: The main purpose for developing artificial intelligence is ________ rather than ________ (simple sentence) ________, we will lose a good opportunity. ________ (complex sentence)

Student 5: Artificial intelligence will make our brains lazy before most of us realize it. First, ________ (any sentence type) Second, ________ (any sentence type) In conclusion, ________ (simple sentence)

3. Write an essay with the title "Should We Have Faith in the Kindness of Strangers?" Then revise your essay by referring to the instructions below.

(1) If you have used compound sentences, underline them.
(2) If you have used complex sentences, underline them.
(3) If you have used compound-complex sentences, underline them.
(4) Are there any imperative sentences, interrogative sentences or exclamatory sentences? If so, what are their functions?

NOTES

Unit 4

How to Use Effective Sentences?

Highlights of this unit:

1. Defining an effective sentence
2. Understanding the criteria of effective sentences: unity, coherence, conciseness, emphasis and variety

Text A

The Beautiful Ferrera

Beth Bowyer

The bright young star of *Ugly Betty* is a real beauty.

A Picture a young woman with unattractive glasses, thick eyebrows and a smile that reveals a mouth full of **braces**. This description can't fit the lead character in a popular TV series, can it? Well, it can! And it does.

B Meet America Ferrera, star of the hit American comedy-drama *Ugly Betty*. Ferrera **portrays** plain Betty Suarez, a hard-working assistant at a fashion magazine. Even though Betty is surrounded by models, her inner beauty more than makes up for her imperfect appearance. Her good heart — and her refusal to be something she's not — allows her to succeed.

C In real life, the beautiful Ferrera is **adored** by fans and critics alike. She won major awards for her *Ugly Betty* performance last year.

D Born in Los Angeles in 1984 to **Honduran** parents, Ferrera is the youngest of six children. Ferrera knew from age 7, when she landed a role in a school play, that she wanted to be a performer. Her mother, however, insisted that America pursue other interests. She didn't doubt her daughter's talent but worried that an acting career wouldn't be easy for a young **Latina.**

E Ferrera didn't allow her mother's worries to stop her, and in 2002, at age 17, she got her first big break. That year, she won a part in a Disney Channel dance movie called *Gotta Kick It UP*! Then in 2005, Ferrera starred in the coming-of-age movie *The Sisterhood of the Traveling Pants.*

F But she didn't become a big star until 2006 when she found success as "ugly" Betty. The show has opened doors for Ferrera — doors that were closed to Latina actresses in the past. Ferrera's next film project is the sequel to the *Sisterhood* movie, which opens in theaters later this year.

G Similar to her Betty character, Ferrera makes no apologies for not being the "perfect size." Happy with her body, she serves as a positive role model for young girls.

H Ferrera truly shines as a positive example for both women and minorities. With her one-of-a-kind appeal, Ferrera keeps *Ugly Betty* fans coming back for more. "I'm so happy and humbled to be on a show that's not only fun... but is making a difference and inspiring people," she says.

New Words and Expressions

braces	*n.*	牙箍（矫正牙齿的钢丝套，尤为儿童所用）
portray	*v.*	（在戏剧等中）扮演某人或表现某事物
adore	*v.*	热爱；爱慕；敬仰
Honduran	*adj.*	洪都拉斯的
Latina	*n.*	拉丁女子
sequel	*n.*	（小说、电影等的）续篇，续集

I Learn from the text

1. Find examples in the text that meet the following requirements.

Sentences that begin with a verb:

____

____

____

Sentences that begin with a preposition:

____

____

____

Sentences that begin with an adjective phrase:

____

____

____

2. Fill in the blanks to complete the sentences. Review the text and check your answers. Discuss the functions of the words or phrases you write.

(1) ________ Betty is surrounded by models, her inner beauty more than makes up for her imperfect appearance.

(2) Ferrera knew from age 7, ________ she landed a role in a school play, ________ she wanted to be a performer.

(3) Her mother, ________, insisted that America pursue other interests.

(4) She didn't doubt her daughter's talent ________ worried that an acting career wouldn't be easy for a young Latina.

(5) I'm so happy and humbled to be on a show ________ is not only fun... but is making a difference and inspiring people.

II Learn to know

Defining an effective sentence

A correct sentence is not necessarily effective. The criteria of an effective sentence include unity, coherence, conciseness, emphasis and variety. In the following examples, which sentences are more effective?

(1) * a. *In real life, the beautiful Ferrera, as the youngest of six children in her family, is adored by fans and critics alike.*

b. *In real life, the beautiful Ferrera is adored by fans and critics alike.*

(2) * a. *Ferrera is the most beautiful actress.*

b. *Ferrera is the most beautiful actress in her fans' eyes.*

(3) * a. *She didn't doubt her daughter's talent and worried that an acting career wouldn't be easy for a young Latina.*

b. *She didn't doubt her daughter's talent but worried that an acting career wouldn't be easy for a young Latina.*

(4) * a. *Even though Betty is surrounded by models, Betty's inner beauty more than makes up for Betty's imperfect appearance.*
b. *Even though Betty is surrounded by models, her inner beauty more than makes up for her imperfect appearance.*

Sentence b of each group is more effective. The problem in the first sentence of each group is as follows: Sentence (1) a fails to maintain unity: "as the youngest of six children in her family" has little to do with the meaning of the main clause; the grammar of Sentence (2) a is correct, but the meaning is not complete; the conjunction "and" of Sentence (3) a makes the meaning illogical, so it is not coherent; in Sentence (4) a, the second and third "Betty" can be replaced by a pronoun to avoid redundancy.

Criteria of effective sentences

Criterion	Definition	Implementation
Unity	All elements of a sentence should be logically connected, expressing a single complete idea.	(1) Do not include information in a sentence unrelated to its main idea. (2) Make sure the information in a sentence has adequate context.
Coherence	Coherence occurs when all the parts and ideas fit together in a reasonable, natural way.	(1) Ensure logical relation in meaning. (2) Ensure agreement in structure.
Conciseness	Conciseness involves using as few words as possible to express the idea fully.	(1) Avoid using a clause if a phrase will do. (2) Avoid using a phrase if a word will do.
Emphasis	To help make a sentence clear and effective, certain words or phrases may naturally receive added stress.	(1) Put key information in the main clause. (2) Use short sentences to show emphasis. (3) Consider using... (4) Consider using...
Variety	Sentence variety is attained by using varied sentence structures and lengths.	(1) Begin sentences with different forms. (2) Vary sentence lengths. (3) Vary sentence types as long as the meaning is properly expressed.

Ⅲ Learn to do

1. Keeping in mind what makes a sentence effective, revise the following.

(1) She is the tallest girl.

____

____

____

(2) The police arrested the criminal and the hostage was saved.

____

____

____

(3) Be slow to promise and quick in performing.

____

____

____

(4) In my opinion, English is more than a tool for communication.

____

____

____

(5) He has tasted all kinds of dishes around the world, and he says the dishes cooked by her mother are the best.

____

____

____

2. Combine the sentences of each group into one.

(1) Ferrera portrays plain Betty Suarez. Betty Suarez is a hard-working assistant at a fashion magazine.

____

____

____

(2) Ferrera was born in Los Angeles in 1984 to Honduran parents. She is the youngest of six children.

____

____

____

(3) Ferrera didn't allow her mother's worries to stop her. In 2002, at age 17, she got her first big break.

____

____

____

(4) The show has opened doors for Ferrera. The doors were closed to Latina actresses in the past.

____

____

____

(5) Ferrera's next film project is the sequel to the *Sisterhood* movie. It opens in theaters later this year.

____

____

____

3. Answer the following questions with sentences that meet the given requirements.

(1) Who is your idol? (Use a coherent sentence that tells who and why.)

____

____

____

(2) What is beauty, in your view? (Use at least one connective word properly.)

____

____

____

(3) What does fashion mean to you? (To add variety, make a sentence that begins with words or phrases as modifying elements other than the subject.)

____

____

____

(4) Why do people tend to follow fashion? (Make sure your sentence maintains unity.)

____

____

____

(5) How do you keep yourself from getting "out of date"? ((Put what is emphasized at the end of the sentence.)

____

____

____

Text B

Ambition

Joseph Epstein

A It is not difficult to imagine a world short of ambition. It would probably be a kinder world: without demands, without **abrasions**, without disappointments. People would have time for reflection. Such work as they did would not be for themselves but for the collectivity. Competition would never enter in. Conflict would be eliminated, tension become a thing of the past. The stress of creation would be at an end. Art would no longer be troubling, but purely **celebratory** in its functions. Longevity would be increased, for fewer people would die of heart attack or stroke caused by **tumultuous** endeavor. Anxiety would be extinct. Time would stretch on and on, with ambition long departed from the human heart.

B Ah, how **unrelievedly** boring life would be!

C There is a strong view that holds that success is a myth, and ambition therefore a **sham**. Does this mean that success does not really exist? That achievement is **at bottom** empty? That the efforts of men and women are of no significance alongside the force of movements and events? Now, not all success, obviously, is worth esteeming, nor all ambition worth cultivating. Which are and which are not is something one soon enough learns on one's own. But even the most **cynical** secretly admit that success exists; that achievement counts for a great deal; and that the true myth is that the actions of men and women are useless. To believe otherwise is to take on a point of view that is likely to be **deranging**. It is, in its implications, to remove all motives for competence, interest in attainment, and regard for **posterity**.

D We do not choose to be born. We do not choose our parents. We do not choose our historical epoch, the country of our birth, or the immediate circumstances of our upbringing. We do not, most of us, choose to die; nor do we choose the time or conditions of our death. But within all this realm of choicelessness, we do choose how we shall live: courageously or in **cowardice**, honorably or dishonorably, with purpose or in drift. We decide what is important and what is trivial in life. We decide that what makes us significant is either what we do or what we refuse to do. But no matter how indifferent the universe may be to our choices and decisions, these choices and decisions are ours to make. We decide. We choose. And as we decide and choose, so are our lives formed. In the end, forming our own destiny is what ambition is about.

New Words and Expressions

abrasion	*n.*	损耗
celebratory	*adj.*	庆祝的，快乐的
tumultuous	*adj.*	欢腾的，热烈的
unrelievedly	*adv.*	持续不变地，未缓解地
sham	*n.*	骗局
at bottom		实际上，根本上
cynical	*adj.*	愤世嫉俗的
derange	*vt.*	打乱
posterity	*n.*	子孙后代
cowardice	*n.*	怯懦

Ⅳ Learn to know more

1. Parallelism to add power to sentences

Text B is rich in parallel structures, which is one reason that the essay is a classic. For example:

*It would probably be a kinder world: **without demands, without abrasions, without disappointments.***

*Such work as they did would **not be for themselves but for the collectivity**.*

*We do not choose **our historical epoch, the country of our birth, or***

the immediate circumstances of our upbringing.

But within all this realm of choicelessness, we do choose how we shall live: ***courageously or in cowardice, honorably or dishonorably, with purpose or in drift.***

A typical type of sentence that employs parallelism is a balanced sentence. In structure, a balanced sentence has parallelism on the level of clause; in function, it is to emphasize particular ideas, to make meanings clear, as well as to create pleasing rhythms.

Examples in advertising:

Light is faster, but we are safer. (Global Jet Airlines' advertising slogan)

Buy a bucket of chicken and have a barrel of fun. (KFC's advertising slogan)

Examples in literature:

Every man has a right to utter what he thinks truth, and every other man has a right to knock him down for it. (*The Life of Samuel Johnson* by James Boswell)

... *and though the mother* was found to be intolerable, and the younger sisters not worth speaking to, a wish of being better acquainted with them was expressed towards the two eldest. (*Pride and Prejudice* by Jane Austen)

2. Inverted sentences to emphasize

An inverted sentence is a sentence in a normally subject-first language **in which the predicate** (verb or auxiliary verb) comes before the subject (noun or pronoun). Often, inverted sentences begin with negative adverbs for emphasis. For example:

...; ***nor*** *do we choose the time or conditions of our death.*

Never *has there been so much protest against the reform.*

Little *does he realize how important the meeting is.*

Seldom *did we eat outside when we were in the countryside.*

Rarely *does he mingle with other students on campus.*

Hardly *ever have there been so many choices for young people entering the work force as there are today.*

Inversion after other adverbs:

Downstairs *ran the Giant in great joy, and out into the garden.*

Up *jumped the frog.*

So *good was the performance that the audience burst into applause after a short silence.*

Only *when you get along with her for some time can you appreciate her character.*

3. Ellipsis in sentences for conciseness

Conflict would be eliminated, tension become a thing of the past.

Now not all success, obviously, is worth esteeming, nor all ambition worth cultivating.

In the first sentence, "would" is omitted before "become." In the second sentence, "is" is omitted after "nor."

In linguistics, ellipsis means leaving out words rather than repeating them unnecessarily. In Chinese, repetition is often used as a cohesive device, but in English, if not for rhetorical effect, it should be avoided, especially in one sentence. For example:

Some books are to be tasted, others to be swallowed, and some few to be chewed and digested; that is, some books are to be read only in parts; others to be read, but not curiously; and some few to be read wholly, and with diligence and attention.

Reading makes a full man; conference a ready man; and writing an exact man.

4. "It" as a formal subject to avoid top-heaviness

It is not difficult to imagine a world short of ambition.

To avoid top-heaviness, "it" is used to take the place of the subject, while the real subject (infinitive, gerund phrase or nominal clause) is postponed.

More examples:

It *is not rare or astonishing to hear that people around us have had operations on their faces or bodies.*

It *is our capabilities and credentials that determine whether we lose or win.*

V Learn to do more

1. Create your own sentences by imitating the following sentence structures.

(1) A body without knowledge is like a house without foundation. (... without... is like... without...)

____

____

(2) Only when you can find peace in your heart can you maintain good relationships with others. (Only when... can...)

____

____

(3) They learn French and we, English. (They... and we, ...)

____

____

(4) It is easier to lose friends than to make them. (It is easier to... than to...)

____

____

2. Here are some opinions given by students when they talk about plastic surgery. Elaborate on the following sentences to make them more effective and informative, following the example given.

Student 1: You will probably first think of a Hollywood star.
When you hear about plastic surgery, you will probably first think of a Hollywood star trying to delay the effects of aging.

Student 2: It is not difficult to find some classic cases.

____

____

____

Student 3: Many people are pleased with the results.

____

____

____

Student 4: Many people suffer more from a psychological problem.

____

____

____

Student 5: People should know the standard of beauty.

____

____

____

3. Write an essay with the title "Is Plastic Surgery a Blessing or Curse?" Then revise your essay by referring to the questions below.

(1) Is your topic sentence concise and relevant?
(2) What connective words or phrases are used to establish coherence?
(3) How do you stress your key points?
(4) Are there any sentences that fail to meet the criteria of effective sentences?
(5) What are the main strengths and weaknesses of your essay?

NOTES

Unit 5

What Is a Paragraph?

Highlights of this unit:

1. Definition of a paragraph
2. Basic structure of a paragraph
3. Paragraph unity

Text A

Sportsmanship

A Sportsmanship by definition is a "fair and generous behavior or treatment of others." Good sportsmanship is characterized by such essential qualities as generosity, respect, commitment and dedication. A child can learn generosity or kindness from adults such as parents and coaches. Whenever it is possible, parents should explain to their children that it is acceptable to not succeed at every activity because there is no growth without failure. Parents ought to inspire children to lose with dignity and win with **humility**. For instance, when a child loses a competitive activity, rather than **having a temper tantrum**, throwing equipment around, and getting angry at the players, they should acknowledge the winner and respectfully accept their loss. On the other hand, when a child wins a game, they should be humble about the victory instead of rubbing it in the opposing team's faces.

B Good sportsmanship means respect. One can show respect to coaches, players, officials, and the game itself by being polite and **courteous**. Just as the Golden Rule goes, treat others the way you would like to be treated. Displaying respect in a sport or any activity is the beginning of establishing positive peer relationships, which is necessary for people to be successful in different aspects of life. To be respectful in a sport is to accept **constructive** criticism rather than make excuses and tear down their teammates. Athletes with good sportsmanship should show their respect to others and the game.

C Good sportsmanship features commitment and dedication. Commitment is the inner drive to put heart and soul into accomplishing your goals. Ultimately, when people make goals for themselves, they are helping pave a path to success. Dedication is the will to work on achieving goals that one has set for oneself. In order to achieve that goal, a person needs to be loyal and diligent. Whenever a team sees that a person has been practicing and trying to make his or her sports career a success, they empathize with and respect the individual. Commitment and devotion as a whole shows how a person has respect for him- or herself, the team, and the game.

D To be successful in a sport, an athlete needs to have good sportsmanship. First and foremost, always congratulate the winning team even if it is not yours. Secondly, show respect to others, whether they are your teammates, officials, coaches, or the opposing team's coaches and members. Finally, always be committed and dedicated to yourself, the sport, and your teammates by showing respect, always making room for improvement, and achieving the goals set for yourself and your team.

New Words and Expressions

humility	*n.*	谦逊
have a temper tantrum		发脾气
courteous	*adj.*	有礼貌的；谦恭的
constructive	*adj.*	建设性的；有助益的
empathize	*v.*	有同感；起共鸣

I Learn from the text

1. Look at Paragraphs B and C of this essay, and identify the sentence that you think expresses the central idea of each paragraph.

____

____

____

2. Tick the sentences that give a detailed explanation of the central idea in the third paragraph.

☐ Good sportsmanship features commitment and dedication.

☐ Commitment is the inner drive to put heart and soul into accomplishing your goals.

☐ Ultimately, when people make goals for themselves, they are helping pave a path to success.

☐ Dedication is the will to work on achieving goals that one has set for oneself.

☐ In order to achieve that goal, a person needs to be loyal and diligent.

☐ Whenever a team sees that a person has been practicing and trying to make his or her sports career a success, they empathize with and respect the individual.

☐ Commitment and devotion as a whole shows how a person has respect for him- or herself, the team, and the game.

3. Look at the third paragraph. What function do you think the last sentence has?

____

____

____

II Learn to know

1. Definition of a paragraph

A paragraph is a group of closely related sentences that deal with a central idea in an organized and coherent way. A good paragraph should include a topic (what the paragraph is about) and a focus (what the specific perspective on the topic is). All of the sentences within a paragraph should be related to the topic and focus.

Text A is a good example. All of the paragraphs in this text are closely related to the same topic, "sportsmanship," but with different focuses. Paragraph A introduces sportsmanship as the essay's main idea and outlines some of sportsmanship's primary qualities; Paragraph B explains in detail how to show respect as one of the features of good sportsmanship; Paragraph C illustrates with examples how commitment and dedication are prominent features in good sportsmanship; Paragraph D, the essay's conclusion, explains why good sportsmanship is needed.

2. Basic structure of a paragraph

In formal academic English, an effective paragraph typically has three principal components: the topic sentence for stating the main idea of the paragraph, supporting sentences for explaining or illustrating the main idea, and the concluding sentence for summarizing or restating the main idea.

• The topic sentence

A topic sentence is generally a one-sentence statement about the main idea of the paragraph and tells readers what the paragraph will be about. Although the topic sentence may appear anywhere in a paragraph, it usually comes at the beginning of the paragraph because it gives readers a sense of what to expect as they read and how the paragraph will be developed. For example, Text A consists of four paragraphs. Both Paragraphs B and C have their first sentence as their topic sentence respectively, "Good sportsmanship means respect." and "Good sportsmanship features commitment and dedication."

A good topic sentence is characterized by the following:

- It identifies the main idea of the paragraph and clearly shows where the paragraph is heading.
- It is balanced — neither too specific nor too general. For example, the sentence "Clouds are white." is probably too specific as a topic sentence because this is an obvious fact which leaves little room for future explanation.
- It hooks the readers.
- It typically does not take the form of an announcement, such as "I want to discuss environmental pollution in this paragraph," because the existence itself of the paragraph evidences the writer's intention or desire (so an explicit announcement then sounds unsophisticated and immature), and, more importantly, a topic sentence of this type lacks focus (a perspective on the topic).

• **Supporting sentences**

The supporting sentences of a paragraph explain and elaborate on the main idea presented in the topic sentence. They answer questions — who? what? where? when? why? and how? — and flesh out the main idea.

Look at Paragraphs B and C in Text A. The first sentence is the topic sentence, and all other sentences act to support this sentence. In Paragraph B, the supporting sentences explain how good sportsmanship requires respect. In Paragraph C, they elaborate on how "commitment" and "dedication" apply to good sportsmanship.

The main types of information in supporting sentences include:

- explanations
- facts
- descriptions
- reasons
- examples
- definitions

Look at the following paragraph.

> Going to college can be expensive. First, college tuition and room and board can cost anywhere from $2,000 to more than $10,000 per semester. Other expenses make going to college even more expensive. For example, books typically cost between $100 and $500 each term. Second, materials are also very expensive. Paper, notebooks, writing utensils, and other supplies required often cost more at the college bookstore than at any local discount department store. For instance, a package of notepaper costing $2 at a discount store might cost $5 at a college bookstore. Finally, there are all kinds of special fees added onto the bill at registration time. A college student might have to pay a $50 insurance fee, a $20 activity fee, a $15 fee to the student government association and anywhere from $500 to $100 for parking. There is another fee if a student decides to add or drop classes after registration. The fees required to attend college never seem to end.

In this paragraph, the supporting sentences include explanations, facts and examples to elaborate on the topic sentence "Going to college can be expensive."

• The concluding sentence

The concluding sentence is typically the last sentence of a paragraph which summarizes or wraps up the paragraph (sometimes there is no concluding sentence). It reiterates the paragraph's main idea and signals to readers that the discussion of that particular idea has been completed. In effect, a concluding sentence ties everything — the topic sentence and the supporting details — together. Paragraphs B and C in Text A are good examples.

Let's see how a concluding sentence might look in the following paragraph:

> The impact of multilingualism can be observed in even more fields. A doctor who can communicate with his or her patients in their native tongue is much more likely to correctly diagnose their problems. A scientist or engineer capable of explaining his findings and ideas to his peers will be able to expedite and improve their work, even if his peers cannot understand him in his first language. Any competent hiring manager in any company in the world will tell you that the ability to speak a foreign language is a prized commodity. Learning to communicate fluently in multiple languages provides additional job security and advancement opportunities.
>
> — By Leonardo De Valoes

The concluding sentence — "Learning to communicate fluently in multiple languages provides additional job security and advancement opportunities." — summarizes the main idea in the paragraph as presented by the topic sentence, "The impact of multilingualism can be observed in even more fields." Notice how the concluding sentence is similar to, but not exactly the same as, the topic sentence.

The following is a checklist for the structure of a paragraph.

Topic sentence	• Summarizes the main idea of a paragraph. • Introduces the topic to be discussed and suggests how the topic will be developed in the paragraph.
Supporting sentences	• Give details about the idea presented in the topic sentence. • Answer questions — who? what? where? when? why? and how?
Concluding sentence	• Restates the main idea using different words from the topic sentence. • Does not introduce new ideas or topics.

Ⅲ Learn to do

1. Judge whether the following sentences make good topic sentences and give your reasons.

(1) George Washington was born in 1732.

(2) George Washington, born in 1732, was one of the most influential politicians in American history.

(3) I am going to discuss World War I.

(4) There are two reasons why some people like to read e-books and two reasons why others like paper books.

(5) Martin Luther King, Jr., was a successful leader because his actions had long-lasting effects, including significantly advancing civil rights.

2. Write a good topic sentence to begin each of the following paragraphs. Remember to include both a topic and a focus.

(1) ____________________

It produces changes in the parts of the brain that regulate stress and anxiety. It can also increase brain sensitivity for the hormones serotonin and norepinephrine, which relieve feelings of depression. Additionally, exercise can increase the production of endorphins, which are known to help produce positive feelings and reduce the perception of pain. Interestingly, it doesn't matter how intense your workout is. It seems that your mood can benefit from exercise no matter the intensity of the physical activity.

(2) ____________________

To begin with, it increases your heart rate, which promotes the flow of blood and oxygen to your brain. It can also stimulate the production of hormones that can enhance the growth of brain cells. Moreover, the ability of exercise to prevent chronic disease can translate into benefits for your brain, since its function can be affected by these diseases. Exercise has been shown to cause the hippocampus, a part of the brain that's vital for memory and learning, to grow in size. This serves to increase mental function in older adults.

(3) ____________________

Regular physical activity can increase the production of hormones that make you feel happier and help you sleep better. It can also improve your skin's appearance, help you lose weight and keep it off, and lessen the risk of chronic disease. Whether you practice a specific sport or follow the guideline of 150 minutes of activity per week, you will inevitably improve your health in many ways.

— By Arlene Semeco

3. Each topic sentence is followed by three supporting sentences that provide relevant, on-target support and three that do not. Write the letters of the three relevant supporting sentences in the spaces.

(1) **Topic sentence: Online shopping may cause people to spend more money.**

A. Nowadays, online shopping is expanding with such e-commerce sites as Taobao, Amazon and eBay.

B. It's much easier to spend money that you don't physically have.

C. The lower price and free shipping encourages you to buy items you may not necessarily need.

D. We can shop when we're tired, we can shop when we're emotional, and we can shop instantly.

E. Some products might only be available for the lower price when you buy them with another product or, just like free shipping, when you spend a certain amount.

F. Online shopping has now become a fashion.

Items that logically support the topic sentence: ______ ______ ______

(2) **Topic sentence: Computers have affected our lives in many ways.**

A. For instance, cars, space exploration equipment, huge industrial machinery, and so on, are designed on computers.

B. Traffic lights that control city traffic are run by computers.

C. Like other computers, smart phones have benefited our lives in various ways.

D. Communication is faster and more convenient than ever due to computers, via the Internet, connecting us with friends and family around the world.

E. Computer users need to understand what they want to accomplish before they can take full advantage of a computer's capabilities.

F. Nowadays, most people have one or more computers: laptops, tablets and/or smartphones.

Items that logically support the topic sentence: ______ ______ ______

(3) **Topic sentence: Artificial intelligence is taking over the workplace.**

A. Already, artificial intelligence (AI) machines can do many tasks where learning and judgment is required, including autonomously driving a car, stock trading, accounting, and many tasks in healthcare.

B. Advances in artificial intelligence will transform our world.

C. For instance, planes are being flown much of the time on automatic pilot.

D. Technological change may eliminate specific jobs, but it has always created more in the process.

E. And the complex problem of controlling air traffic around large modern airports is also achieved by artificial intelligence that operates well beyond the capability of mere human air traffic controllers.

F. There will be an increasing number of jobs related to programming, robotics, engineering, etc.

Items that logically support the topic sentence: ______ ______ ______

NOTES

Text B

Sportsmanship and the Game of Life

A Sportsmanship relates to life in numerous ways — for example, earning a big promotion over a coworker, winning a game against a rival team, or triumphing in an election. Children are shown at young ages how to be respectful and be productive in life. "Tough" and "unfair" are two words that people often use to describe life. Like life, sports can also be tough and unfair. Sports can be a wonderful training ground for life's challenges. Failures in sports, as in life, should not discourage a competitor, but further motivate him or her. Those who work hard, respect others, and are dependable are more likely to become successful in life. Ultimately, there is no success without failure. Failures can help one figure out where to improve and so eventually succeed.

B Like in sports, everyone experiences failure in life; even people who invent things that we use on a day-to-day basis cannot avoid failure. Thomas Edison was asked if he felt like a failure for not being able to create a successful light bulb after 9,000 failed attempts. Edison answered, "Young man, why would I feel like a failure? And why would I ever give up? I now know definitively over 9,000 ways that an electric light bulb will not work. Success is almost in my reach." As a result of 9,000 trials and errors, Edison invented the light bulb. Our greatest successes in life are not the ones that come easily but the ones we have to work the hardest to achieve. We are often inspired by those who have faced the most difficult of life's challenges and have still maintained dignity and grace.

C Even though sportsmanship is expected mostly in sports, it can also be practiced in a work environment. Sportsmanship is an important characteristic in employees, who should endeavor to be respectful, fair, and gracious toward their boss, coworkers, and the workplace itself. Employees demonstrate sportsmanship by treating everyone with respect, always trying their best, and being reliable.

D In short, like in sports, there are many ways one can feel they are winning in life. Oftentimes, being humble is better than being arrogant and proud. Although there may be uncomfortable encounters with those who have not succeeded as you have, nothing is gained by being self-centered and **ungrateful**. Good sportsmanship is, in many cases, an important part of being successful. Being generous, fair, hardworking, and respectful are all life-winning characteristics of sportsmanship.

New Words and Expressions

coworker	*n.*	同事
triumph	*n./v.*	胜利
productive	*adj.*	多产的；富有成效的
dependable	*adj.*	可靠的
gracious	*adj.*	和蔼可亲的；有礼貌的
ungrateful	*adj.*	不感激的

IV Learn to know more

• Unity

As explained in Text A, a paragraph usually opens with a topic sentence, followed by supporting sentences that illustrate the main idea stated in the topic sentence, and closes with a concluding sentence that paraphrases the main idea. This is called the unity of a paragraph. In other words, a unified paragraph introduces one idea, supports it with explanations or illustrations, and completes it with a conclusion.

Take the last paragraph of Text B as an example. The first sentence is the topic sentence stating the central idea. The following three sentences provide sufficient and persuasive information to support the idea presented by the topic sentence. Then the last sentence echoes the topic sentence as a summary of the whole paragraph.

Look at one more example below:

(1) Generally, language has three functions according to its purpose: informative, expressive and directive. (2) Firstly, speaking to communicate information fulfills the informative function. (3) Secondly, speaking in order to express feelings and attitudes of the listener demonstrates the expressive or emotive function. (4) And finally, speaking in order to make other people act fulfills the directive function. (5) Thus, on different occasions, people use language for different purposes according to these three functions.

This is a unified paragraph with a clear and logical organization. In this paragraph, Sentence (1) introduces the main idea as the topic sentence. Sentences (2)–(4) are supporting sentences that elaborate on the idea expressed in Sentence (1). Sentence (5) is the concluding sentence that summarizes the previous four sentences.

V Learn to do more

I. Identify the unrelated sentences that do not belong to the original paragraphs and underline them.

(1) Learning a foreign language helps improve memory. A recent study published in the *Journal of Experimental Child Psychology* aimed to find out what effect learning a foreign language had on a child's memory. This study found that bilingual children performed much better than monolingual children on tasks using their working memory. (Working memory deals with the storage and processing of information over a short period of time.) The conclusion of the study was that knowledge of more than one language had contributed to their better working memory. Speaking two languages, and switching between them, makes you better at multi-tasking, too.

(2) Being able to speak another language can help you make better decisions. Studies from the University of Chicago have shown

that people who speak another language are better able to pick up nuances and subtleties in any given situation. The benefits of multiple languages can start as early as before a baby is able to speak. A heightened appreciation of the complexities of a situation can lead to more rational decision-making in many areas of life. Monolingual people, on the other hand, tend to base their decisions more on emotions. In other words, speaking another language can improve your life through better decision-making.

(3) In fact, as crazy as it may sound, learning a foreign language can actually increase the size of your brain. Speaking more than one language provides constant exercise for your brain. And keeping your brain active is one way in which to delay the onset of dementia. A group of Swedish scientists did an MRI study which showed that certain parts of the brain were bigger in people who had learnt a foreign language. In this study, two groups of subjects underwent brain scans. One group did an intensive language course for three months. The other, the control group, did intensive courses in a subject that was not a language. What the scientists found was that specific parts of the language learners' brains became bigger than those of the non-language learners.

2. Write a paragraph of 150 words about sportsmanship with special reference to a sports star you like most. Then check your writing with your classmates according to the checklist given.

Topic sentence:

____

____

____

Supporting sentences:

____

____

____

Concluding sentence:

____

____

____

Paragraph Writing Criteria Checklist

	Yes	No
• My paragraph begins with a sentence that clearly states the topic.		
• All subsequent sentences clearly support the topic.		
• Transitions between sentences are smooth and clear.		
• My closing sentence restates the main idea in the opening sentence.		
• I have used language appropriate for the topic.		
• I have checked all words for accuracy and spelling.		
• I have checked punctuation for accuracy.		
• Grammar is appropriate and accurate.		

NOTES

Unit 6

How to Write a Coherent Paragraph?

Highlights of this unit:

1. Definition of paragraph coherence
2. Cohesive devices
3. Writing skills for coherent paragraphs

Text A

Chinese Dream, the People's Dream and the World's Dream

A In China, the "Chinese Dream" has become a hot topic for discussion. From state leaders to ordinary citizens, from people's everyday conversations, writings submitted to online forums, and comments on Weibo, Chinese people have never been more excited about dreams than they are today. And the "Chinese Dream" has also caught the attention of the rest of the world. If you google the phrase "Chinese dream" you get about 287 million results in less than a second. The *Financial Times* of the UK has commented: "The dream of China not only concerns China's destiny but also the world's destiny." This begs the question — How does the "Chinese Dream" relate to the rest of the world?

B Firstly, the "Chinese Dream" is a dream of peaceful development. The "Chinese Dream" has arisen in parallel with peaceful development and can only come true through peaceful development. The aims of the "Chinese Dream" are not to conquer, surpass or replace anyone, but to provide Chinese people with better education, more stable job opportunities, improved incomes, higher levels of medical and health services, and a more beautiful environment. China clearly opposes **hegemony** and power politics, devotes itself to building a peaceful and stable international environment, promotes peaceful settlements of international disputes and hotspot issues, improves international and regional security cooperation, and seeks to achieve collective security, common security and cooperative security.

C Secondly, the "Chinese Dream" is the dream of win-win cooperation. China is an active advocate and practical actor of win-win cooperation. Since China's accession to the WTO, it has imported 687 billion dollars' worth of goods per year and has created more than 14 million jobs for related countries and regions. China has driven one fourth of global economic growth and made universally acknowledged contributions to world economic recovery after the International Financial Crisis in 2008. In the next five years, China will import 10 trillion dollars' worth of goods. The scale of its **outbound** investment will reach 500 billion dollars. And more than 400 million overseas trips will be made by Chinese tourists. Thomas L. Friedman, columnist of *The New York Times*, even says you can only see the future in China. Certainly, during the process of realizing its own dreams, the cooperation path between China and the world will be increasingly expanded and the pragmatic collaborations between China and other countries will be solidly advanced. The "Chinese Dream" will create more cooperative opportunities for China and the world, more **convergence** of common interests, and more benefits for the people in all countries.

D Thirdly, the "Chinese Dream" is also a dream of openness and inclusiveness. The policy of cutting China off from the outside world came at a heavy price. Today's China has realized more than ever the importance of embracing the world with an open attitude. The "Chinese Dream" not only belongs to China, but also the whole world. We will not close our doors to keep our "Chinese Dream" to ourselves, but we'll share the "Chinese Dream" with the world to deepen reform and further open up. In pursuing the "Chinese Dream," we will not shut ourselves up, but take full advantage of international talents, technology, resources, capital and markets, further integrating into the world and creating opportunities for the common development of the world.

E While 1.4 billion Chinese people are striving for the realization of the "Chinese Dream," the international society is also spending **unremitting** efforts to realize the dream of the world — building a world with lasting peace and common prosperity. The "Chinese Dream" is **inseparable** from the world's dream. The "Chinese Dream" will bring to the world new hope, new opportunities and new driving forces.

New Words and Expressions

hegemony	*n.*	霸权
outbound	*adj.*	对外的
convergence	*n.*	趋同性
unremitting	*adj.*	不停的；不懈的
inseparable	*adj.*	不可分割的

I Learn from the text

1. What are special features of this essay regarding the use of words and grammatical structures?

____

____

2. Why do you think the words "Chinese Dream" are repeated in this essay?

____

____

3. Do you think Paragraph C is organized in a coherent way? Explain why or why not.

____

____

II Learn to know

1. Coherence

Paragraph coherence means that every sentence in a paragraph "sticks together," linking together in continuous lines of thought. Coherence is achieved when sentences are well connected and arranged so that the ideas expressed in the paragraph flow smoothly from one to another in a logical sequence.

For example, in the second paragraph of Text A, coherence is achieved because each sentence within this paragraph is closely related to each other. The first sentence, the topic sentence, expresses the basic idea that "the 'Chinese Dream' is a dream of peaceful development." The next sentence explains why the "Chinese Dream" is indeed a dream of peaceful development. The third sentence further elaborates on the aim of the "Chinese Dream" with regard to peaceful development. The final (fourth) sentence enumerates what actions China is taking and will take to advance peaceful development. Therefore, this paragraph coherently focuses on and expands its main idea, as stated in the topic sentence.

2. Cohesive devices

When writing, there are a number of cohesive devices, which can be classified into lexical and syntactic categories that help achieve coherence in a paragraph.

- **Repeat key words or phrases**

Repeating key words or phrases is a way of knitting sentences in a paragraph together. This important device connects sentences and focuses the reader's attention on a central idea. For instance, in the fourth paragraph of Text A, the author repeats "Chinese Dream" five times to emphasize the main idea of the Chinese Dream as a dream of openness and inclusiveness, thereby helping coherently organize the paragraph.

Consider another example:

> We Americans are a charitable and humane people: we have institutions devoted to every good cause from rescuing homeless cats to preventing World War III. But what have we done to promote the art of **thinking**? Certainly we make no room for **thought** in our daily lives. Suppose a man were to say to his friends, "I'm not going to **PTA** tonight (or choir practice or the baseball game) because I need some time to myself, some time to **think**"? Such a man would be shunned by his neighbors; his family would be ashamed of him. What if a teenager were to say, "I'm not going

to the dance tonight because I need some time to **think**"? His parents would immediately start looking in the **Yellow Pages** for a psychiatrist. We are all too much like Julius Caesar: we fear and distrust people who **think** too much. We believe that almost anything is more important than **thinking**. (Carolyn Kane, from "Thinking: A Neglected Art." *Newsweek*, December 14, 1981)

PTA: 家长教师会

Yellow Pages: 分类商业电话号码簿

In this paragraph, the author uses three forms of the same word — **think**, **thinking**, **thought** — to link the different examples and reinforce the main idea of the paragraph.

- **Use pronouns to link sentences**

Pronouns are often used to refer to a noun or noun phrase in a preceding sentence, so using pronouns is a simple and natural device to link sentences through reference. For example, in the third paragraph of Text A, the sentence "Since China's accession to the WTO, it has imported..." employs the pronoun "it" in the main clause to refer to "China" in the "since"-phrase. This kind of substitution is often used in English writing. The following paragraph shows how the use of different masculine pronouns link one sentence to another to avoid unnecessary repetition.

Richard Wagner was a monster of conceit. Never for one moment did **he** look at the world or at people, except in relation to **himself**. He was not only the most important person in the world to **himself** in **his** own eyes; **he** was the only person who existed. **He** believed **himself** to be one of the greatest dramatists in the world, one of the greatest thinkers, and one of the greatest composers. To hear **him** talk, **he** was Shakespeare, and Beethoven, and Plato rolled into one.

— from *The Monster* by Deems Taylor

- **Use synonyms, hyponyms or superordinates to link ideas and add variety**

Synonyms, hyponyms and superordinates provide alternative word choices that can add variety to a paragraph and help eliminate unnecessary repetition.

Look at the following example.

Titanic was one such disastrous story. One of the nicest and most beautiful vessels in its century, it embarked on its maiden voyage to America, but a dire event awaited the ship. The luxurious ocean liner struck a floating mountain of ice and soon thereafter sank.

The paragraph above achieves coherence by, in part, using synonyms such as ***disastrous*** and ***dire***, and hyponyms such as ***ship***, ***ocean liner***, and ***Titanic*** that relate to the superordinate *vessel*, all of which avoids monotonous repetition by allowing the author to vary the phrasing.

- **Use transitional expressions to connect ideas and sentences**

Transitional expressions are words or phrases that are used to establish the logical connection between a sentence and the one before it. They serve as signals to show how the previous ideas are connected to what follows, so the reader can easily understand the relationship between them. The most common transitional expressions are listed below:

LOGICAL RELATIONSHIP	TRANSITIONAL EXPRESSION
Similarity	also, in the same way, just as, likewise, similarly
Contrast	but, however, in spite of, on the one hand… on the other hand, nevertheless, nonetheless, notwithstanding, in/by contrast, on the contrary, still, yet, while
Sequence/Order	first(ly), second(ly), third(ly), …, last(ly), next, then, finally
Time	after, afterward, at last, before, currently, earlier, immediately, later, meanwhile, now, recently, simultaneously, subsequently, then
Example	for example, for instance, namely, specifically, to illustrate
Emphasis	especially, even, indeed, in fact, in particular, of course, particularly, truly
Place/Position	above, adjacent, below, beyond, here, in front, in back, nearby, there
Cause and Effect	accordingly, as a result, consequently, hence, so, therefore, thus
Additional Support or Evidence	additionally, again, also, and, as well, besides, equally important, further, furthermore, in addition, moreover, then
Conclusion/Summary	finally, in a word, in brief, briefly, in conclusion, in the end, in the final analysis, on the whole, thus, to conclude, to summarize, in sum, to sum up, in summary

• **Use parallel structure.**

Parallel structure involves repeating grammatical constructions to connect ideas that have a similar nature or importance. When done well, it adds clarity and increases readability by creating patterns readers can follow more easily.

In Paragraph B of Text A, for example, the author uses parallel structure to concisely highlight similarities between ideas, which in turn helps make the paragraph more coherent.

> The aims of the "Chinese Dream" are not to **conquer, surpass or replace** anyone, but to provide Chinese people with **better education, more stable job opportunities, improved incomes, higher levels of medical and health services,** and a **more beautiful environment.** China clearly **opposes** hegemony and power politics, **devotes** itself to building a peaceful and stable international environment, **promotes** peaceful settlements of international disputes and hotspot issues, **improves** international and regional security cooperation, and **seeks** to achieve collective security, common security and cooperative security.

Ⅲ Learn to do

I. Fill in each blank in the paragraph below with one transitional word or phrase from the table.

for instance	although	whereas	another	for example
first	in contrast	additionally	while	lastly

(1) ________ American and British English may seem quite similar on the surface, on closer inspection, there are significant differences in vocabulary, grammar, spelling and pronunciation. (2) ________, the most noticeable difference between American and British English is vocabulary. There are hundreds of everyday words that are different. (3) ________, Americans go on *vacation*, (4) ________ the British go on *holiday*. New Yorkers live in *apartments*, while Londoners live in flats. (5) ________, there are a few grammatical differences between the

two varieties of English. (6) ________, in American English, collective nouns are considered singular (e.g., The band is playing). (7) ________, collective nouns can be either singular or plural in British English (e.g., "The band are playing." or "The band is playing.") (8) ________ difference between American and British English relates to spelling. In American English textbooks, they talk about red *color*, (9) ________ in British textbooks it is spelled as red *colour*. (10) ________, the most significant difference between the pronunciations of British and American English is the way the letter "r" is pronounced. In British English, when "r" comes after a vowel in the same syllable (as in *car*, *hard*, or *market*), the "r" is not pronounced, while in American English the "r" is usually pronounced.

2. Compare the following paragraphs. Decide which one is more coherent and give your reasons.

The Great Wall of China is one of the greatest wonders of the world. The Great Wall of China was listed as a World Heritage by UNESCO in 1987. It is like a gigantic dragon. The Great Wall winds up and down across deserts, grasslands, mountains and plateaus. It stretches 21,196 kilometers from east to west across China. The Great Wall is a Chinese icon. It reflects China's national pride, the country's traditions of grand projects, and determined resistance. It shows us China's extravagant architecture and creativity.

The Great Wall of China, one of the greatest wonders of the world, was listed as a World Heritage by UNESCO in 1987. Just like a gigantic dragon, it winds up and down across deserts, grasslands, mountains and plateaus, stretching about 21,196 kilometers from east to west across China. The Great Wall is a Chinese icon. It reflects not only China's national pride, the country's traditions of grand projects and determined resistance, but also China's extravagant architecture and creativity.

3. Judge whether the following paragraphs are sufficiently coherent or not. If not, make them more coherent by using cohesive devices.

(1) College graduates are more likely to experience job satisfaction. A 2016 Pew Research report found that 77% of workers with a

postgraduate degree and 60% of workers with a bachelor's degree believe their job gives them a sense of identity, versus just 38% of those with a high school diploma or less. Workers with a bachelor's degree or more advanced education are also significantly more likely to say their job is a career, with 70% viewing their job as a career compared to just 39% of workers with no college education. (By Susan Bogle)

(2) People sometimes procrastinate on tasks. People are optimistic about their ability to complete those tasks in the future. Students might decide to postpone getting started on assignments that are due a few weeks from now. Students feel that there will be plenty of time to get it done later. In many cases, this form of optimism might occur. They underestimate the time it will take to complete the tasks in questions. This phenomenon is known as the planning fallacy. It can lead both procrastinators as well as non-procrastinators to assume that they will finish upcoming tasks faster than they actually will.

NOTES

Text B

Chinese Dream and American Dream

A The Chinese Dream and the American Dream have a lot in common despite their many differences. Both dreams consist mainly of hopes for **prosperity** and happiness for their respective nations and citizens. The Chinese government and the American government want their countries to enjoy good fortune and success. Success is a high **priority** in these countries because citizens who work hard help make the nation a better place to live in. Another similarity is that both countries want a better life for their citizens, who believe that if they generate wealth for their nation, then status and wealth will accrue to them in return. China and America have been attempting to build and fulfill their dreams for many years. Different Presidents and Chairmen have altered the vision depending on what is best for their country and people. Even though both countries have different forms of government, and different cultures and beliefs, they both want their nations and citizens to have better, more virtuous lives.

B Although some national dreams may be similar to others, no two are 100% alike. China believes strongly in unity, as well as in national prosperity, national **rejuvenation**, collective harmony and happiness, the wisdom of the group, and united effort. Citizens in China who contribute to the nation are awarded and praised because they want the nation to improve as a whole, and are not just seeking their own betterment. Chinese citizens and the government are working hard to make China more united and more prosperous. On the other hand, America firmly believes in individualism. Most individuals work hard to be successful and have a good life. The Dream in America differs by age group because the "American Dream" has changed dramatically through the years. In the past, the American Dream often included wanting a big family, a beautiful home, a luxurious vehicle, and the **trendiest** clothes, but these goals have shifted in the 21st century. Americans today simply want to be successful enough to provide for themselves and their families without relying on others, to attend university, to have a stable career, and to give back to the community. Americans in the 21st century are not as materialistic as they were in the past. The American and Chinese Dreams have different histories, which helps explain the different ideas about what the Dreams should be.

C In the final analysis, China and America have common beliefs when it comes to prosperity and working hard to achieve success. Nonetheless, the two countries have different cultures, which have spawned separate Dreams that differ in emphasis. China is a united nation, so citizens heavily rely on one another to build a better nation. By contrast, America stresses being independent and **self-sufficient,** so citizens focus more on their own personal success rather than the nation's success. Even though the dreams differ, both countries rely on their citizens to pursue the national "Dream" and in turn help the nation prosper.

New Words and Expressions

prosperity	*n.*	繁荣
priority	*n.*	最重要的事
rejuvenation	*n.*	恢复活力
trendy	*adj.*	时髦的
self-sufficient	*adj.*	自给自足的

Ⅳ Learn to know more

Two common methods for developing paragraphs are "comparison and contrast" and "cause and effect." The following are some writing skills for developing such paragraphs.

1. A comparison and contrast paragraph

A comparison discusses how two or more elements are similar, while a contrast looks at how two or more elements are different. A comparison and contrast paragraph, then, analyzes two subjects by comparing them, contrasting them, or doing both. For example, Paragraph B in Text B is a contrast paragraph because it discusses the differences between "Chinese Dream" and "American Dream." Well-reasoned, well-written comparisons and contrasts lend tremendous coherence to paragraphs. A typical comparison and contrast paragraph can be written as follows:

- **Begin by choosing two comparable subjects that connect in a meaningful way.**

Make sure the subjects are comparable. Comparing a baby and a tree would probably not work, but comparing Richard Nixon and Barack Obama would likely be more productive. In both comparison and contrast, the two subjects should to a certain degree relate to each other, sharing some common characteristics.

- **Identify the comparable points between the two subjects, and brainstorm a list of similarities and differences.**

A Venn-diagram is a good way to display similarities and differences. Take the comparison of bears and birds as an example, which is shown in the diagram below. The elements of mode of movement, type of bodily cover, behavior in winter, and variety of vocalization are organized in the Venn diagram to illustrate similarities and differences between the two kinds of animals.

Venn-Diagram

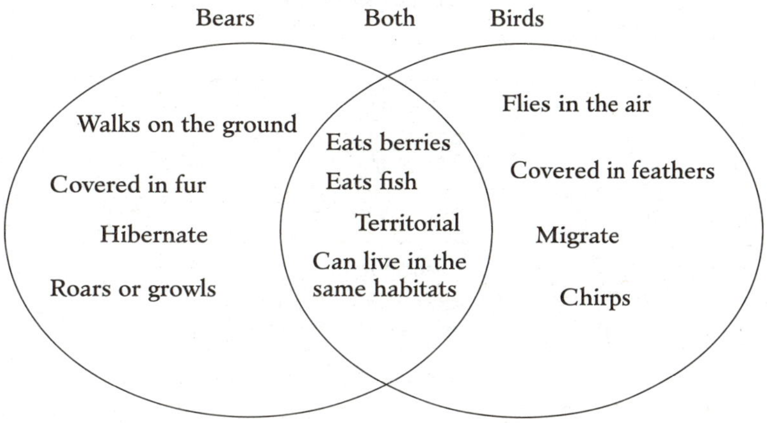

- **Write a topic sentence to show the comparison or/and contrast between the subjects as a controlling idea.**

The topic sentence should include the topic that shows the writer's intention to compare and/or contrast, and expresses the main idea of the paragraph. For birds and bears, the topic sentence could be: "Even though bears and birds have something in common, they differ greatly in four aspects."

- **Explain every contrast and comparison in complete and detailed sentences. Use transitional expressions to achieve greater coherence.**

Write supporting sentences to provide relevant and detailed information about each comparable point. Transitional expressions will improve coherence in the paragraph overall, making it read more smoothly and logically.

There are mainly two ways to write a comparison and contrast paragraph: the subject-by-subject method and the point-by-point method. In a subject-by-subject paragraph, one subject is fully discussed, and only then is the second subject discussed. In a point-by-point paragraph, by contrast, each point as it applies to each subject is discussed before moving to the next point.

Transitional Expressions Used for Comparison and Contrast

Comparison	Contrast
too	although
also	but
the same	however
both, neither	unlike
like	whereas
likewise	while
similarly	yet
just as	conversely
in addition	in/by contrast
as well as	on the other hand
in the same way	nevertheless
in a similar way	on the contrary

- **Write a concluding sentence to summarize the whole paragraph.**

2. A cause and effect paragraph

A cause and effect paragraph is written to discuss why something occurs (the cause) and what happens as a result (the effect). A cause and effect paragraph can focus on causes, effects, or both. There are two main ways to write a cause and effect paragraph.

• **(1) Start with a cause followed by one or more effects.**

A cause and effect paragraph may start with a topic sentence that describes a cause. Then it continues by explaining the effects. The following paragraph, in which "AB" denotes a generic country or region, is a good example:

> The fertility rate rose 7% in Western AB between 1990 and 2010 [the cause]. One effect of this has been increased pressure on food resources [Effect 1], since agricultural productivity has remained the same. A second and related effect has been the lowering of the overall standard of living in Western AB [Effect 2]. We can expect this to eventually lead to amigration from rural areas to the cities [Effect 3]."

• **(2) Start with an effect followed by one or more causes.**

A cause and effect paragraph can, alternatively, start with a topic sentence that describes an effect. Then it describes the cause(s). Study the following example.

Those with a college degree are shown to earn a million dollars more over a lifetime than those who do not go to college at all [the effect]. One reason why this is so is the higher paying jobs available to college graduates [Cause 1]. Another reason is that college graduates are more comfortable with high-technology, which helps them start high-profit businesses [Cause 2].

Transitional Expressions to Achieve Coherence

Cause	Effect
because	so
since	thus
for	hence
as	therefore

续前表

Cause	Effect
due to	consequently
as a consequence of	as a consequence
on account of	for this reason
as a result of	as a result

V Learn to do more

I. Following the guidelines discussed above, write a short comparison and contrast essay about Beijing and Shanghai.

Step 1: Brainstorm

(1) List attributes or qualities of two topics in the circles, placing any shared qualities in the overlapping section. Be specific and include as many details as you can think of.

(2) Identify the most important qualities in each circle and match at least three opposing aspects "between the two topics."

Fill out the Venn-diagram with your ideas.

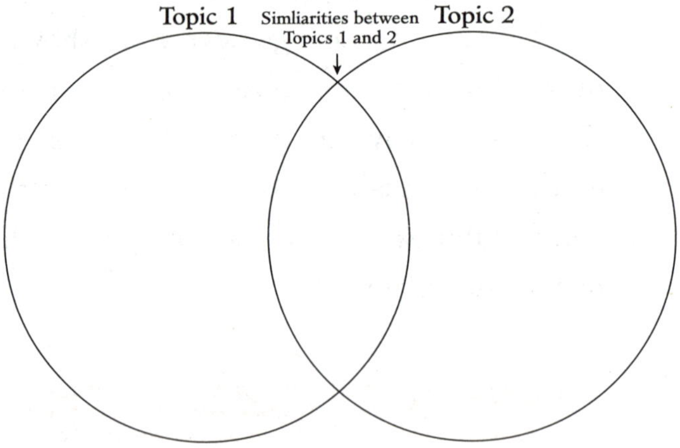

Step 2: Complete the following tables according to the information in your diagram.

Subject-by-Subject Structure

	Comparison/ Contrast 1	Comparison/ Contrast 2	Comparison/Contrast 3
Subject 1			
Subject 2			

Point-by-Point Structure

	Subject 1	Subject 2
Comparison/Contrast 1		
Comparison/Contrast 2		
Comparison/Contrast 3		

Step 3: Choose either of the two paragraph structures and complete the following information.

1) Topic: ______________________________

2) Comparable points: ______________________________

3) Topic sentence: ______________________________

____

____

____

4) Supporting sentences:

____

____

____

5) Concluding sentence:

____

____

____

6) Transitional expressions:

____

____

____

2. Choose one topic from the list below and develop a cause and effect paragraph.

A. What causes fast food to be popular? / What are the effects of this popularity?
B. The Internet's influence on kids
C. Growing up in poverty
D. Social media's effect on young people
E. Effects of online dating
F. What causes a person to lie, and what are the effects of telling lies?
G. How traveling the world affects one's life and personality?
H. The reasons for (causes) and results (effects) of pursuing higher education
I. The causes and/or effects of racism
J. The causes and/or effects of procrastination

NOTES

Unit 7

What Is an Essay?

Highlights of this unit:

1. Definition of an essay
2. Organization of an essay
3. Types of essays

Text A

The Palace Museum

A Established in 1925, the Palace Museum is located in the **imperial** palace of the Ming (1368–1644) and Qing (1644–1911) dynasties. In 1961, the State Council designated the former imperial residence as one of China's foremost-protected cultural heritage sites, and in 1987 it was listed as a UNESCO World Heritage site. The magnificent architectural complex, also known as the Forbidden City, and the vast holdings of antiquities make it one of the most **prestigious** museums in China and the world.

B Situated in the heart of Beijing, the Palace Museum is approached through the Gate of Heavenly Peace, Tian'anmen. Immediately to the north of the Palace Museum is Prospect Hill (also called Coal Hill), while on the east and west are the Wangfujing and Zhongnanhai neighborhoods. Ancient China's astronomers endowed the location with cosmic significance. They correlated the emperor's residence, which they considered the **pivot** of the Earth, with the Pole Star — believed to be the center of the heavens. Because of its centrality and restricted access, the palace was called the Forbidden City. It was built from 1406 to 1420 by the third emperor of the Ming Dynasty, the Yongle Emperor who determined to move his capital northward from Nanjing to Beijing.

During nearly six hundred years of imperial operation, the palace served as the residence and court of twenty-four emperors.

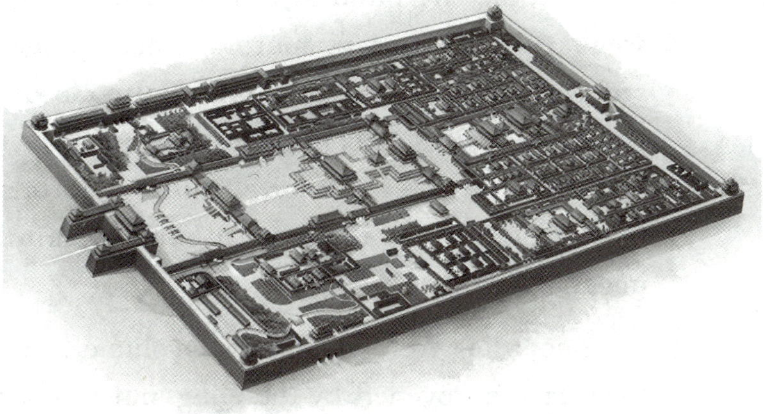

C The Forbidden City is surrounded by 10-meter-high walls and a 52-meter-wide **moat**. Measuring 961 meters from north to south and 753 meters from east to west, the complex covers an area of 1,120,000 square meters. Each side of the rectangular city has a gate. These four gates are the Meridian Gate (Wu Men) on the south, the Gate of Divine Prowess (Shenwu Men) on the north, and the East and West Prosperity Gates (Donghua Men and Xihua Men), respectively. Entering from the south, visitors will see a succession of halls and palaces spreading out on either side of the central axis. The **glowing** yellow roofs of the stately buildings seem to rise above the **vermilion** walls. This magnificent sight is amplified by the painted ridges and carved beams of the ancient structures.

D Known as the Outer Court, the southern portion of the Forbidden City features three main halls — the Hall of Supreme Harmony (Taihe Dian), Hall of Central Harmony (Zhonghe Dian), and Hall of Preserving Harmony (Baohe Dian). Mirroring this arrangement is the Inner Court, which is the northern portion of the Forbidden City. The Palace of Heavenly Purity (Qianqing Gong), Hall of Union (Jiaotai Dian), and Palace of Earthly Tranquility (Kunning Gong) lie upon the central **axis**. The Six Eastern Palaces and the Six Western Palaces are private imperial residences found on their respective sides of the main axis. The Inner Court is not only comprised of the residences of the emperor and his consorts but also venues for religious rituals and administrative activities. The far north end of the Inner Court is the Imperial Garden.

E In total, the buildings of the two courts account for an area of some 163,000 square meters. These structures were designed in strict accordance to the traditional code of architectural hierarchy, which designated specific features to reflect the paramount authority and status of the emperor. Ordinary mortals were forbidden — and most would never dare — to come within close proximity to this imperial city.

F According to a twenty-eight volume inventory published in 1925, the treasure trove left by the Qing imperial family numbered more than 1,860,000 items. This collection included ancient jade artifacts from the earliest dynasties of Chinese history; paintings and calligraphy dating to as early as the seventh century; **porcelain** from the Song and Yuan; gold and silver **ornaments**; antiques made of bamboo, wood, horn, and gourds; religious statues in gold and bronze; thousands of imperial robes and ornaments; textiles; and furniture. In addition, countless books, literary works, and historical documents were found among the antiquities. All these were divided into separate collections that were placed under the care of designated staff. Exhibition halls were opened to display some of the treasures.

G Although the Forbidden City used to be an **impenetrable** fortress, the imperial palace is now a public museum. With rich collections representing the broad spectrum of 5,000 years of Chinese civilization and the 600-year history of the Forbidden City, the Palace Museum has seen many developments since its founding in 1925 and looks forward to carrying on the legacy of the past for future generations. Now, as always, the Palace Museum is committed to the preservation of national heritage and the goal of serving as a model for museums around the world.

New Words and Expressions

imperial	*adj.*	帝王的，皇家的
prestigious	*adj.*	享有声望的
pivot	*n.*	中枢，中心人物
moat	*n.*	护城河
glowing	*adj.*	发光的
vermilion	*adj.*	朱红色的
axis	*n.*	中轴线
porcelain	*n.*	瓷器
ornament	*n.*	饰物
impenetrable	*adj.*	不可进入的，不能穿过的

I Learn from the text

1. What is the purpose of this essay?

____

2. How many parts can this essay be divided into?

____

3. What do you think are the functions of each part of the essay?

____

II Learn to know

1. Definition of an essay

An essay is a short literary composition based on a single subject matter, and it often gives the personal opinion of the author. A famous English essayist, Aldous Huxley, defines an essay as, "a literary device for saying almost everything about almost anything." *The Oxford Dictionary* describes it as "a short piece of writing on a particular subject." Text A takes *The Palace Museum* as its subject matter and describes the place in detail from different perspectives. Actually, the function of an essay depends upon the subject matter and whether the writer wants to describe, persuade, explain, or inform.

2. Organization of an essay

A typical essay is composed of a **title, introduction, body and conclusion**. It can be either one paragraph or several, depending on the amount of material covered as well as on the writer's intention.

- **Title**

A clear and well-considered proper title can convey to readers the main idea at first sight. However, sometimes, a rhetorical title, such as a question or idiom, can draw a reader's attention and interest him or her in reading the article. A good title is half the success of the essay.

The title of Text A is "The Palace Museum," which puts forward directly the subject matter and suggests that the author will focus on one or more aspects of the museum.

- **Introduction**

An introduction, or introductory paragraph, starts an essay. It is also called "the gateway" to an essay because it attracts the attention of readers and gives them background on the topic. It also introduces the thesis statement of the essay, which is the heart of an essay, and indicates what is to come in subsequent paragraphs.

A major purpose of an introduction is to make readers feel that they are going to read a well-organized piece. In other words, an introduction levels the groundwork before the "real" essay begins.

The first paragraph of Text A introduces the Palace Museum, including its location and importance as part of China's and the world's cultural heritage. In the later paragraphs, the museum is described in detail.

- **Elements of an introduction**

Generally, an introduction has three elements which usually come in a sequence, one after another. They are:

- Hook or attention grabber
- Background information
- Thesis statement

Hook: A hook is the first sentence of an introduction. It is also called an "attention grabber." As the name suggests, it is intended to hook readers, or grab their attention, to encourage them to read the entire piece. A hook could be a provocative quote, a relevant verse, or an anecdote about an interesting incident or situation.

For example, in Text A, the first sentence mentions the year the museum was established, as well as the fact that it resides on a centuries-old site. It invites readers to think about the museum — its historical and cultural significance.

Background Information: Background information takes most of the space in an introduction. It normally comes after the hook, which usually is just a single sentence. By contrast, background information, in even a short essay, can take three to four sentences, and more in a longer essay. Its purpose is to give readers some context, so that they have an idea what comes next and can better understand it.

The second sentence in Paragraph A feeds readers background information — China's and the world's recognition of the importance of The Palace Museum.

Thesis Statement: This element is often called the heart, core, or central point of the essay. It informs readers what the writer's focus is, and what approach the essay is going to take. Without a thesis statement, readers may not clearly grasp what an essay is about. In a five-paragraph essay, the thesis statement should require only a single sentence, with three points of evidence to be discussed later in body paragraphs. However, in longer essays, the thesis may be spread through two or three sentences, with each sentence having two or three points: pieces of evidence, arguments, or counterarguments.

The last sentence in Paragraph A serves as the thesis statement. It announces the importance of the museum as one the most prestigious in China and the world.

• Body

The body of an essay comes between the introduction and the conclusion. The body is the most important part in an essay because it presents evidence to support opinions and try to convince the reader if the aim is to persuade, or it presents explanations and details if the aim is to inform.

A body may consist of more than one paragraph, each elaborating a single idea supporting the thesis statement. In a five-paragraph essay, there are three body paragraphs, while in longer essays there could be five or more. In major research papers, there may be hundreds of body paragraphs.

In Text A, the body is composed of Paragraphs B–F. Each of these paragraphs introduces a specific aspect of the museum. For example, Paragraph B looks at some of the history of the museum.

The most important thing in the body is to explain and offer supporting details. An explanation or example often starts with "in other words," "it means," "for example," "for instance," etc. The goal is to use different words to explain something further or in a fresh way, so that readers understand better.

For instance, the topic sentence of Paragraph F is "The treasure trove left by the Qing imperial family numbered more than 1,860,000 items." This tells us that this paragraph mainly talks about the holdings of the museum. In order to explain further and support the topic sentence, the author adds "The collection included ancient jade artifacts from the earliest dynasties of Chinese history; paintings and calligraphy dating to as early as the seventh century," and so on.

Supporting details include concrete examples, rather than just explanations or general examples. A supporting detail can be just an example from everyday life, or quotes from reputable sources and statistics from research studies.

In Text A, Paragraphs B–F each contain concrete examples (comparisons) and statistics supporting the thesis statement. For example, in Paragraph C, the author details the perimeter and extent of the museum. The statistics offered amply support the thesis statement in Paragraph A: "The magnificent architectural complex, also known as the Forbidden City, and the vast holdings of antiquities make it one of the most prestigious museums in China and the world."

• **Conclusion**

A conclusion is typically the last paragraph of an essay, coming after the body paragraphs. A conclusion should summarize the key points and finish the essay on a strong note. If the goal is to persuade, the main arguments should be reiterated and/or main evidence reviewed; if the objective is to inform, the most important aspects of the subject may be again cited or the reason why the overall topic matters may be revisited.

A conclusion is comprised of three important elements. They are **a rephrasing of the thesis statement, a summary of the main ideas, and concluding remarks.**

Rephrasing the thesis statement reminds readers of the essay's main topic. It is not uncommon for the re-statement of the thesis to be spread over two or three sentences, with the thesis' main points expanded for effect.

The Summary of main ideas should cover all of the main points of the essay, which usually requires three or more sentences. These main points may actually be some or all of the ones in the thesis re-statement earlier in the conclusion, repeating them for emphasis. Normally, however, these main points are other than the ones given in the thesis statement.

The concluding remarks close the essay. They could be a call to action, a suggestion or recommendation, a warning, a final question demanding further response or investigation, or just a statement to wrap up the whole enterprise.

In Text A, Paragraph G works as the conclusion of the essay. Its first sentence acknowledges the major change in the way the place is used. The second sentence summarizes the main points of the essay, and in the last sentence, the author echoes the first paragraph by stating the Palace Museum's value both to the nation and to the world — preserving national heritage and serving as a model for museums around the world.

In summary, the components of an essay are listed in the table below:

	Components
(1) TITLE	
(2) INTRODUCTION	Hook
	Background Information
	Thesis Statement
(3) BODY	Specific Ideas
	Explanations/Examples
	Supporting Details
(4) CONCLUSION	Rephrasing of the Thesis Statement
	Summary of the Main Ideas
	Concluding Remarks

Ⅲ Learn to do

1. Read the passage below and decide which of the following is the best title for it.

- ☐ Three kinds of loneliness
- ☐ Loneliness and social contacts
- ☐ Loneliness and disease
- ☐ Chronic loneliness

Most people feel lonely sometimes, but it usually only lasts between a few minutes and a few hours. This kind of loneliness is not serious. In fact, it is quite normal. For some people, though, loneliness can last for years. Now researchers say there are three different types of loneliness.

The first kind of loneliness is temporary. This is the most common type. It usually disappears quickly and does not require any special attention. The second kind, situational loneliness, is a natural result of a particular situation — for example, a family problem, the death of a loved one, or moving to a new place. Although this kind of loneliness can cause physical problems, such as headaches and sleeplessness, it usually does not last for more than a year.

The third kind of loneliness is the most severe. Unlike the second type, chronic (长期的) loneliness usually lasts more than two years and has no specific cause. People who experience habitual loneliness have problems socializing and becoming close to others. Unfortunately, many chronically lonely people think there is little or nothing they can do to improve their condition.

Psychologists are trying to find ways to help habitually lonely people for two reasons: such people are unhappy and unable to socialize, and there is a connection between chronic loneliness and serious illness such as heart disease. While temporary and situational loneliness can be a normal, healthy part of life, chronic loneliness can be a very sad and sometimes dangerous condition.

2. Read each of the four paragraphs below. Mark "C" if it would best serve as a conclusion, "I" if as an introduction, and "B" if as a body paragraph.

______ Material possessions bring convenience, leisure, and comfort to our lives. Television provides us with entertainment; cars provide us with convenience; a nice home provides a warm shelter and comfort. Even though most of these are things we could live without, we have to admit that they brighten up our lives a little.

______ In conclusion, material possessions make our lives better — not to mention that, in most societies, it's considered better to own more. And lastly, it feels good to own something. Therefore, I think that material possessions make life easier and more convenient and they make us happy as well!

______ It's a joyful feeling when you own something. It may be a cute adornment; or it may be a grand mansion. Either one is precious to you, and you value and take care of it. The responsibility you feel for taking care of the possession itself makes it special. So, even if they may at times be a bit troublesome, material possessions still make you happier.

______ Nowadays, material possessions play a large part in our lives. While some may doubt that they really do make us happy, I argue that they make life easier and more convenient, as well as making people happier. Firstly, they provide us with a more comfortable and leisurely life. Secondly, in most societies, people believe that the more possessions you have, the better. It's a great feeling to possess something, especially when it is precious to you.

Text B

Live and Work in China

A Every day, China is becoming more and more influential in terms of the global economy, international politics. The time when China was an underdeveloped country passed long ago, and nowadays this Asian giant is a recognized and respected partner of other powerful countries such as the United States and Russia. Although not all of the regions of China are as remarkably **prosperous** as its coastal areas, China has recently become incredibly attractive for millions of people around the world as a place to live and work — for a number of reasons.

B China has a rapidly growing economy, with many companies — for example, Meizu, Xiaomi, AliExpress, and many others — now becoming world leaders in their industry, or at least major competitors of existing leaders. This means two things: firstly, China has a giant labor market, with the number of workplaces growing every day. For a person inside or outside China, this is a great opportunity to find his or her dream job. Secondly, a person from abroad looking for an **internship** or a job in China has a better chance of being hired in China than of being hired for the same kind of position in his or her home country due to the person's expertise and knowledge of English (or another foreign language), which can **theoretically** help a Chinese company become a more efficient competitor. This factor can also lead to quicker promotions, so many are embracing the opportunity. Working in China is a great experience, and a huge bonus to one's **CV** no matter where one works after one's "Chinese experience."

C If you move to China, you will discover another reason why this country is worth moving to: its prices. For Chinese people, the costs of different products may be high, but if you are a citizen of the United States, the European Union, or any other country with a high quality of life, you will find Chinese prices pleasantly low — the cost of living in China is affordable, even if you are an intern on a student **budget**. See for yourself: public transport is cheap even in Beijing, the capital of China — only $0.32 to get to any corner of the city by subway; taxis are cheap as well. As for the local food, it is not only cheap, but also delicious, so you will find yourself regularly dining in all kinds of street cafes, stands, and so on. A portion of Beijing duck will cost you about $10, and a barbecue on a stick will be only $0.30. Considering that Chinese **cuisine** is as filling as it is tasty, such prices are more than affordable.

D In addition, living and working in China can be a life-changing experience. As a Westerner, you will see more or less similar things, get into similar situations, or meet alike people while you travel around the Western **Hemisphere**. However, arriving in China changes everything. The differences between your mentality and the Chinese mentality can be frustrating sometimes, but when you learn to adjust to **discrepancies**, you will open your mind and truly love the industrious and unusual people of China. You will visit **exotic** places, find yourself in a number of challenging situations, and learn to live in a foreign culture — what can be more enriching in terms of experience?

E China is one of the most rapidly-developing countries in the world. Its culture is different from the Western one, but it is also the number one reason to move to this beautiful country. As a Western person, you will find it beneficial not just in terms of your career (which is not difficult to build there), but also in terms of the cost of living and the limitless new experiences you will gain on a daily basis.

New Words and Expressions

prosperous	*adj.*	繁荣的
internship	*n.*	实习
theoretically	*adv.*	理论上
CV	*n.*	简历
budget	*n.*	预算开支
cuisine	*n.*	烹饪料理
hemisphere	*n.*	（地球）半球
discrepancy	*n.*	差异
exotic	*adj.*	国外的，异域风情的

Ⅳ Learn to know more

An essay can be **descriptive, narrative, expository or argumentative** in nature.

An argumentative essay is different from the three other types mentioned. It is written to discuss a controversial issue and, using clear thinking and reason, convince readers of the validity of the given point of view.

Like the other essays, it may involve three parts:

- Introduction
- Arguments/Counterarguments
- Conclusion

An argument is the main statement in an argumentative essay and usually presents as the central point that the writer develops in order to convince his readers; **a counterargument** is also an argument the writer uses to refute the arguments others posit against the essay's position, giving weight to that position. Arguments and counterarguments may both appear in the body of an argumentative essay.

For example, the author of Text B aims to persuade foreigners to live and work in China, supporting his objective by offering three reasons that foreign people should enrich their lives by starting or continuing their careers in China.

Text B is a typical five-paragraph argumentative essay that can be divided into three parts. The introduction, Paragraph A, puts forward the author's main idea — the thesis. Paragraphs B–D are the body; each paragraph proffers a different argument in support of the thesis, while Paragraph F, the conclusion, brings the essay to a close.

In the introduction, Paragraph A, the author first acknowledges that China has greatly changed. Then, he states his thesis and foreshadows the structure of the essay — that is, he posits that living and working in China is attractive to foreigners for several reasons.

In Paragraphs B–D, the body of the essay, the author details three arguments: taking advantage of China's economic growth, enjoying the relatively low cost of living, and having an exotic experience.

In Paragraph E, which is the conclusion part, the author summarizes his main points and restates his thesis.

A descriptive essay creates a word-picture of a specific person, place, object or even an abstraction, such as an emotion. It tries to make readers feel, smell, see, taste, or hear what is being described. A descriptive essay can be either objective or subjective. When writing a descriptive essay, the writer should select concrete details carefully in order to make his point clear to the reader. Text A is a typical descriptive essay, focusing on a specific place — The Palace Museum; in the body, the writer details different aspects of the museum.

Here is an excerpt from a descriptive essay. The author uses descriptive language to paint a dramatic picture of an encounter with a stranger.

Sample 1:

As I passed through the gates, I heard a squeaky voice. A diminutive middle-aged man came out from behind the trees — the caretaker. He worked a toothbrush-sized stick around in his mouth, digging into the crevices between algae'd stubs of teeth. He was barefoot; he wore a blue batik shirt known as a buba, baggy purple trousers, and an embroidered skullcap. I asked him if he would show me around the shrine. Motioning me to follow, he spat out the results of his stick work and set off down the trail.

A narrative essay is very similar to a descriptive one. The only difference between the two is that the narrative essay tells a story, either in the first person or in the third person. It describes people, their conversations, and their experiences in order to make a point or illustrate a moral principle.

A narrative essay should include the "Six Ws" (sometimes referred to as "Five Ws and How" or "5W1H") — Who, What, When, Where, Why and How — that is, the character(s), the event(s), the time(s), the place(s), the reason(s) or purpose(s), and the process(es).

Sample 2:

When I burst in that afternoon, she was in conference with an executive of the Curtis Publishing Company. She introduced me. He bent low from the waist and shook my hand. Was it true as my mother had told him, he asked, that I longed for the opportunity to conquer the world of business?

My mother replied that I was blessed with a rare determination to make something of myself.

"That's right," I whispered.

"But have you got the grit, the character, the never-say-quit spirit it takes to succeed in business?"

My mother said I certainly did.

In this piece from a narrative essay by Russell Baker, of the famed *Saturday Evening Post*, the author illuminates, through a snippet of dialogue between him and a publishing executive, the efforts of his mother to advance his interests (as she interprets them). The characters and their dialogue are both sharply presented, giving us a clear understanding of the situation.

An expository essay is written to explain or inform — to explicate, illustrate, and/or clarify in a way that helps readers more clearly and deeply understand something. The essay could take the form of an investigation, evaluation, or even argumentation — but whatever the form, the aim is clarity and comprehension. The most common strategies are development by example, definition, comparison and contrast, division and classification, process analysis, and causal analysis.

Sample 3:

The Hong Kong-Zhuhai-Macao Bridge (HZMB) is a mega-size sea-crossing linking Hong Kong, Zhuhai and Macao. It is the longest bridge-tunnel-system sea-crossing in the world, crossing the waters of the Lingdingyang Channel in the Pearl River Estuary. Hong Kong Port has a Passenger Clearance Building with a floor area of over 90,000 square metres and the 12 km Hong Kong Link Road connects the Hong Kong Port to the 29.6 km Main Bridge, which is comprised of a 22.9 km sea viaduct and 6.7 km sub-sea tunnel. After a distance of 41.6 km, the bridge arrives at the Zhuhai Port and Macao Port. From there, the 13.4 km Zhuhai Link Road brings the total length of the HZMB to 55 km.

The table below outlines different essays in terms of purpose and function:

Essays	Purpose	Function
Descriptive	to describe	to present a person, place, or thing in a way that causes readers to feel as if they have personally experienced the subject
Narrative	to tell a story	to present one or more persons' experiences, or recount one or more events, real or imagined
Expository	to explain or inform	to illuminate and clarify ideas, persons, places, etc., through description, process, comparison/contrast, or problem solution
Argumentative	to argue a point of view or discuss a specific issue	to persuade readers by presenting evidence that supports the author's view or that adds context to the issue

V Learn to do more

Bearing in mind the function and components of each part of an essay, read the sample below and answer the questions afterward:

SAMPLE

On College Education

In China overall, people with a formal college education only account for 4% of the population, but for younger generations, a college education is now seen as a must. What is learned at university will be of great help in the job market. The skills gained in college will be useful outside of work, as well. Hence, college represents one of the most important periods of our lives.

In college, we students need to change our approach to learning. In high school, we get used to learning what the teachers push on us. Everything they show us we assume to be correct. But now, we have to reflect on ourselves and find what to learn and how to learn it ourselves.

What's more, because teachers no longer play as central a role, they usually try to improve our critical thinking, which is one of the faculties we students — and, indeed, most adults — sorely need. We are adults and should make our own decisions. We need to let go of outdated ideas and nurture our own creativity.

1. Identify and underline the thesis statement of this writing.

2. Write another body paragraph that looks at a new aspect of the issue, with explanation and supporting details.

3. The conclusion of this sample is missing. Please write a solid and sound conclusion of 3–5 sentences to end this essay.

____

____

____

____

4. In Text B, the author tries to persuade foreigners to reside and work in China. Perhaps you would like to go abroad to study and live. Please write an argumentative essay about studying abroad, adopting a similar structure and method to those used in Text B. Your essay should include three arguments.

____

____

____

____

____

____

____

____

____

____

____

____

____

NOTES

Unit 8

How to Write a Clear Essay?

Highlights of this unit:

1. Organizing and developing an essay
2. Making your essay clear and powerful

Text A

Huawei's Culture Is the Key to Its Success

A Today, Huawei is the only Chinese company — out of the 91 Chinese companies listed on the *Fortune* Global 500 list — earning more revenue abroad than in China. Huawei's revenue from overseas markets exceeded that from the Chinese market for the first time in 2005. In 2012, Huawei surpassed Ericsson — at that time the world leader in telecommunications and networks — in terms of sales revenue and net profit, and this trend continued in the **fiscal year** of 2014 when Huawei reached an all-time high sales revenue of $46.5 billion and net profits of $4.49 billion (both in U.S. dollars).

B What makes it so successful? As the saying goes, "Success has many fathers." But as with many great companies, we find part of the solution to this puzzle by looking at the specific values that define the culture of Huawei. Having interviewed people working for Huawei, reading articles, letters and keynotes by the founder Ren Zhengfei, and finally interviewing Ren Zhengfei himself allowed us to understand the foundation of Huawei's value-driven culture.

Customer-First Attitude

C Strong leaders provide a sense of purpose to their people, and Ren Zhengfei is no exception. His first and foremost concern is the customer. Many companies adopt a customer-focused attitude, but how many of them truly live it? Huawei distinguishes itself from the competition in this regard.

D The example of this customer-first attitude comes from the early episode in their history that's since become something of a company legend. In desert and rural areas in China, rats often **gnawed** the telecom wires, severing customers' connections. The multinational telecom companies providing service at that time did not consider this to be their problem, but rather that of the customer. Huawei, in contrast, viewed the rat problem as one the company had the responsibility to solve. In doing so, they acquired extensive experience in developing **sturdier** equipment and materials — such as chew-proof wires — which helped them later on to gain several big business accounts in the Middle East, where similar problems **stymied** the multinational firms.

E Since then, there have been other projects where Huawei experienced severe climate challenges, such as building the highest wireless communication base station in the world (6,500 meters high on Mount Everest) and building the first GSM network within the **Arctic** circle. Overcoming these challenges has helped the company learn a lot that it can apply to many other situations.

F For example, when Huawei expanded their 3G market in Europe, they noticed that European carriers expected base stations to be more compact, easier to install, greener, and more energy efficient, while offering wider coverage. Based on these customer needs, Huawei became the first company to launch the concept of distributed base stations that enables radio access for large to small private networks. This innovation made it cheaper for carriers to deploy base stations, and was popular with European carriers.

Employee Dedication

G Huawei emphasizes that the only way to obtain opportunities is through hard work. For example, in the early years of the company, every new employee was given a blanket and a **mattress**. Many of them would work late into the night, then sleep in their offices, perhaps taking a catnap during lunch again the next day. As one Huawei employee said: "The pads were to us a representation of hard work in the old days and this idea has now been translated into the spirit of being dedicated to do the best in anything we do."

H Knowing that a dedicated and committed work force makes companies more competitive is not a too difficult concept to understand. The way to develop a sense of dedication in employees — as is the case in Huawei — is, however, a more difficult nut to crack. Huawei does it in part with the type of incentive performance system the company employs. Huawei is not a public company, and is in fact owned by the employees. Ren Zhengfei's shares account for nearly 1.4% of the company's total, and 82,471 employees hold the rest (as stated in Huawei's 2014 Annual Report). This employee shareholding system is referred to within Huawei as the "silver handcuff." It is a system that is different from the more common stock option arrangement, which is often termed the "**golden handcuff**." The idea underlying this scheme is that Ren Zhengfei wants to share both responsibilities and benefits with his colleagues. As he puts it, he wants everyone to act like the boss. Important to note, however, is that only those who perform well enough qualify to participate.

I There's a shared belief within the company that an **IPO** would result in only a few people getting very rich, and the majority losing their motivation. Ren Zhengfei has emphasized that avoiding an **IPO** and hewing to the current employee-ownership structure is what helps the company maintain a strong collective fighting spirit.

J As many people know, Ren Zhengfei is a man with an army background — he served in the People's Liberation Army, an experience he credits for his drive to fight and survive, qualities that are reflected in one of his favorite slogans in the early days of Huawei. So far, Huawei has had many successes to celebrate.

New Words and Expressions

fiscal year		财年
gnaw	*vt.*	咬；啃
sturdy	*adj.*	强壮的；结实的
stymie	*vt.*	妨碍；阻挠
Arctic	*adj.*	北极（区）的
dedication	*n.*	贡献；现身；敬业
mattress	*n.*	床垫
golden handcuff		金手铐；挽留人才的工具和手段
IPO		（公司股票的）首次公开发行；上市

I Learn from the text

1. Work in groups. Read the essay and write an outline of the essay.

INTRODUCTION	
HOOK:	
BACKGROUND INFO	
THESIS STATEMENT	
BODY	
ASPECT 1:	Supporting details:
ASPECT 2:	Supporting details:
CONCLUSION	
RESTATEMENT	

2. Discuss in groups.

Who do you assume are the readers of this essay?

____

____

____

____

What do you think is the author's purpose for writing this essay?

____

____

____

____

What content in the body do you think is more important?

____

____

____

____

What is the function of Paragraph G?

____

____

____

____

II Learn to know

Writing a lucid and powerful essay requires clear thinking and good organization. An essential part of an essay, the thesis statement, sets the course for the rest of the piece. We need to know how to prepare for writing, how to organize our sources and ideas, and how to develop them into an effective essay.

The writing process:

- Clarifying your aim and identifying your readers
- Generating and organizing your ideas
- Drafting your essay
- Revising and editing

We can categorize these four steps into three major procedures — **Before writing**, **While writing** and **After writing**.

1. Before writing — clarifying your aim and identifying your readers

First of all, you should clarify your aim — that is, decide what type of writing you want to do: a narrative, a description, an exposition or an argumentation. To determine what kind of essay you want to write, ask yourself: Do I want to persuade, or inform, or just present my feelings, experiences and/or opinions?

After answering this question, identify the audience you want to reach so that you can determine what tone and style to adopt and what kind of information needs to be included.

Text A is an exposition that was published in *Harvard Business Review*. It is almost 900 words long and is very well-organized. The purpose of the writers is to get across the point that Huawei's culture is a key to its success, as the title suggests. The target readers of the magazine are people in the business world who may not know much or anything about Huawei.

2. Before writing — generating and organizing your ideas

After you have a clear aim and audience in mind, you are ready to move to the next step — generating and organizing ideas.

Step 1 Idea Generation

The well-known process of brainstorming includes the following steps:

- Write down your goals for the essay and any challenges or problems you currently face in writing it.
- Associate your ideas with words, make connections between ideas, and allow your imagination to roam free.
- Create a list of every idea that occurs to you, no matter how silly or stupid they seem.
- After a few hours or a day or two, go back over your list and cross out the ideas you don't like.

Step 2 Idea Organization

Next, you need to arrange your ideas logically — using inductive or deductive reasoning, chronological order, importance order (most to least important, or vice versa), cause-effect relationships, or some other ordering principles. Taking the time to properly outline your essay — idea by idea, paragraph by paragraph — will save time in the end by helping you focus on your writing along a logical path and avoid wasting effort on unproductive points of penetration and dead ends. Being aware of the difference between the Chinese thinking pattern and the English thinking pattern may be helpful, too. In Chinese writing, ideas tend to be organized in a curved pattern, while in English-language writing, ideas tend to be organized in a straightforward pattern.

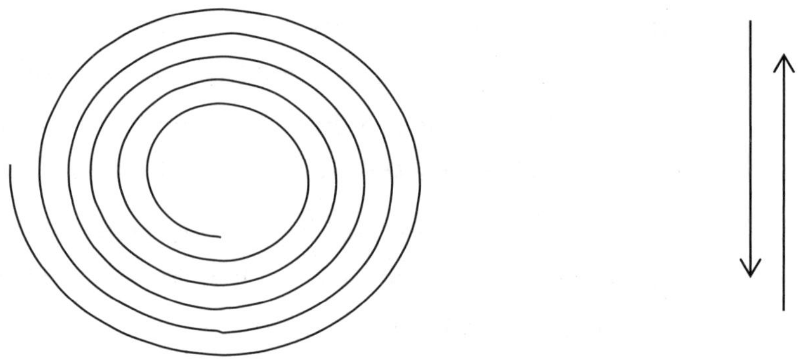

Chinese thinking pattern (curved) English thinking pattern (straightforward)

Robert B. Kaplan, 1966.

In general, as you know, an essay has three parts: the introduction, the body, and the conclusion. The introduction should present your thesis statement. The body can be composed of several paragraphs, each of which needs to support your thesis. Typically, the body contains examples and explanations. The conclusion should be concise, revisiting the thesis and your purpose for writing, and summarizing the main supporting points from the body.

Text A, for example, starts with the introduction of Huawei's profile (Paragraph A) and then poses the question (beginning of Paragraph B) "What makes Huawei so successful?" as the thesis statement. In Paragraphs C through I, the body, the question is answered, with evidence, examples, explanations and details to support the writers' view. The last paragraph, the conclusion, summarizes the main points and restates the thesis of the essay.

3. While writing — drafting a cohesive and coherent essay

Transitional words and phrases — such as "first," "initially," "at the beginning," "second," "third," "then," "furthermore," "in addition," "finally," "in conclusion," and so on — tie ideas together (within sentences, from sentence to sentence, from one paragraph to another) and indicate at what stage your essay is. They are like road signs to direct the reader's thinking. Think of them as bridges that lead from one idea to the next, helping keep your reader on the right path. Here is a list of transitional words you can use when you develop an essay.

Grammatical Devices	Functions for Cohesion
it, this, that	Making references to earlier nouns
either ... or ... neither ... nor but, however, otherwise, rather conversely on one/the other hand	Providing alternatives
and, also, too, in a like manner identically, equally as well as, comparatively correspondingly, by way of comparison	Making comparisons
on the other hand, conversely furthermore, additionally, moreover in addition to, together with	Adding new ideas/Reinforcing already-stated ideas
previously, simultaneously in the first place, at this point first, last, until, in the meantime	Showing chronology
in particular, especially, particularly	Highlighting/Emphasizing
in summary, in conclusion, in short	Concluding and summarizing
in/by contrast, on the other hand, on the contrary, above all, after all	Showing contrast
although, even though, in spite of, despite	Showing concession
for instance, for example	Giving examples
because, because of, so	Giving reasons/causes
finally, as a result (of), consequently, so	Showing results/effects

Cohesion refers to state of connectedness between clauses, sentences and paragraphs in an essay to help the reader understand how parts of the essay fit together. Grammatical devices — including pronouns, transitional expressions, and repetition of key words or phrases, among other things — make it clear how each piece of the text figures into the whole. For example, in the first paragraph of Text A, "at that time" refers to the year 2012 previously mentioned, and "this trend" refers to Huawei's increasing profitability noted in the preceding text. By using *that* and *this*, the text is linked together. Another example appears in Paragraph D: the phrase "the customer-focused attitude" is repeated from Paragraph C, thus connecting the two paragraphs in a coherent way. The following table provides kinds of grammatical devices which can be used to achieve cohesion in a text.

4. After writing — revising and editing

After finishing your first draft, proofread it using the checklist below:

- Topic sentence or thesis statement;
- Ideas organized logically in different paragraphs;
- Supporting details in each paragraph;
- Grammatical devices used to tie clauses, sentences and paragraphs together (cohesion);
- No spelling mistakes, sentence fragments, or punctuation errors.

Peer review is also a very effective way to check your essays. Except for during an exam, of course, you can ask your peers to proofread your work, just as you can offer to proofread theirs.

NOTES

Ⅲ Learn to do

1. The following paragraphs are out of order and some of the cohesive devices are missing. Put the paragraphs in chronological order and fill in the blanks with proper cohesive devices.

How Bricks Are Made
________, the well-blended compound is pressed in a mould or cut by a wire cutter, in order to form brick-shaped pieces. During the next 24–48 hours, dozens of these fresh bricks are kept in a drying room that is actually a large oven.
________, underground clay is dug up as the raw material by a large digger. Clay lumps are then stacked on a metal grid which serves to break up chunks into much smaller pieces. After falling on a roller, the stuff is further conveyed and mixed with sand and water.
________, cooled hard bricks get packed and delivered by trucks to a building site.
________ the bricks are dry, ________ is the heating and cooling process. Bricks are transferred to a so-called kiln, another type of hotter oven, in which they are burned twice, moderately and highly, in temperatures from between 200 °C and 980 °C to between 870 °C and 1,300 °C. Then the heated bricks are deposited in a cooling chamber for two or three days.

2. What do you know about traditional Chinese festivals? Work in a group, brainstorm about activities people do at one of the festivals and research its origin. Then write an exposition introducing the festival. While writing, pay attention to cohesion and coherence.

____

____

____

____

3. Work in a group and read the sample draft below and fill in the outline.

TITLE:	
INTRODUCTION	
THESIS STATEMENT	
BODY	
ARGUMENT 1	Idea:
	Supporting detail:
ARGUMENT 2	Idea:
	Supporting detail:
CONCLUSION	
SOLUTION	
RESTATEMENT	

SAMPLE:

On Paying for Downloaded Music

In recent days, whether downloaded music should be paid for has become a highly debated topic. I think that all of us who download music should pay for it — that is to say, there's no free lunch any more. My reasons are as follows.

Firstly, as far as I am concerned, it's natural to pay for music downloading. If we have to pay for dinner at a restaurant or items at a supermarket, then why wouldn't we pay for downloading music that we enjoy? Artists' work needs legal protection; charging for music helps protect their intellectual property rights. The pirating of music and other forms of creative endeavor seems out of control, but we can see that governmental enforcement of copyrights is gradually becoming more effective. For example, the National Copyright Administration has released an order to online music operators to cease spreading unauthorized music.

Secondly, in my opinion, it's essential to pay for it. Even if a song costs each listener just a small amount, the revenue for the artist and industry can be substantial. I think that profitability is important because it allows the industry as a whole to thrive and improve the quality of its product — music. As long as we want to hear new and beautiful music, we have to be willing to pay for the composers, singers and lyricists who create it.

In conclusion, paying a small fee to download songs from music platforms offers a reasonable way for artists to profit from their art and helps safeguard their intellectual property rights. As long as we have a variety of high-quality music to choose from, I don't mind paying for it.

NOTES

Text B

A Craze for 1,800-Year-Old Fashion

A Like teenagers the world over, Chen Bolin, a Chinese university student, feels a need to belong. Unlike many of his peers, Mr. Chen has found a spiritual home: China of the Wei and Jin Dynasties, about 1,800 years ago. So deep is this bond that on special occasions he wears flowing, wide-sleeved **robes** inspired by third-century dress. One moment of connection stood out, when he wore robes to a museum in Shaoxing, the eastern city where he studies. There he found a sculpture describing **sages** from the Wei and Jin era. His own clothes were "exactly like theirs," he recalls happily. He saluted the statues and told them: "Dear **ancestors**, I've heard so much about you. It is my good fortune to see you today."

B The teenager developed his passion at high school in Pingliang, **perched** in the hills of Gansu, an inland province. Though a rather small spot, Pingliang is home to a traditional culture association. Such clubs are spreading fast.

C Enthusiasts claim that a million Chinese, mostly youngsters, regularly wear Hanfu, or robes inspired by traditional Han dress. Media hail Hanfu as a welcome complement to calls to revive traditional culture and values. In April 2018 the Youth League declared a first "Traditional Chinese Garment Day." The league urged young Chinese to wear ancient finery to demonstrate "cultural confidence" to the world.

D As Mr. Chen shares his story, the slight, bespectacled teenager is wearing robes of lilac and white, **embroidered** with blue clouds, an outfit he says is Jin-Dynasty day-wear. All around are thousands of fellow enthusiasts attending a Hanfu cultural festival held annually in Xitang, a **quaint**, canal-side town near Shanghai.

E Hanfu wearers vary in their devotion to historical accuracy. Mr. Chen has brought along a classmate whose look combines a black-and-white military uniform and 21st-century sneakers. "I think this is Han Dynasty," the classmate mumbles, when asked. The colours are more Ming, says Mr. Chen, gently correcting his friend's dates by about 1,100 years.

F Enthusiasm counts for more than precision. On this sunny festival weekend a local Starbucks boasts staff in toga-like robes, a warrior in chain-mail queuing for coffee, and outside, a Taoist priest in a **cloak** outfit he calls "a bit of messed-up fusion." Luling Manman, an author invited to the festival as an expert on ancient etiquette, defines Hanfu as "all forms of clothes we Chinese people have worn over the course of 5,000 years."

G At the Xitang festival, youngsters have fun. Blushing students **giggle** their way through a lesson in ancient dancing. Earnest, robe-wearing young men take photographs of each other playing the flute or practising archery. Children take part in a fashion show, **swishing** along a catwalk in too-long finery.

H The festival organiser is Vincent Fang Wenshan, a Chinese lyricist behind some of the most famous Mandarin pop songs of recent times. A 49-year-old in black embroidered robes, Mr. Fang urges younger enthusiasts to be open to modernised Hanfu. He sighs that some purists will not tolerate any dress not found in ancient wall paintings, and draws a **wistful** comparison with Japan, where traditional customs and modern culture co-exist easily. Wearing a kimono on a Japanese bus causes no astonishment, notes Mr. Fang, lamenting that a gap of several centuries separates Han traditional culture from the modern world. He would like to see Hanfu fans bridge that gap.

I Historians might quibble with some of Mr. Fang's details. Plenty of traditions actually survived. Look past the costumes and the history, and something simpler appears: a whole country yearning to know where it belongs.

New Words and Expressions

robe	*n.*	长袍
sage	*n.*	贤达
ancestor	*n.*	祖先
perch	*v.*	坐落
embroider	*v.*	刺绣
quaint	*adj.*	古雅的
cloak	*n.*	斗篷；宽大的外衣
giggle	*v.*	咯咯地笑
swish	*v.*	发出嗖嗖的声音
wistful	*adj.*	渴望的

Ⅳ Learn to know more

Making your essay clear and powerful requires thinking about every element: how to keep the readers' attention, starting with the title and an introduction that includes a well-considered thesis statement, working through body paragraphs that support the thesis, and ending with a conclusion that wraps up the whole effort in a sound and solid way.

- **1. Choose a suitable title.**

A title needs to be specific and concise. An overly long title may turn off a reader from the start. Similarly, too short a title may lack enough information to pique someone's interest. Your title needs to embody the main idea of your essay, but if you can do so in an original or creative way, you will have gone a long way toward grabbing and keeping your reader's attention. One technique is to pose a question as a title. Figures of speech can also be adapted as titles.

Text B describes "Hanfu Fever" and a cultural event called the "Xitang Festival," examples the author uses to illustrate Chinese people's connections to their history and culture. However, "Hanfu" might be too strange to Western readers who do not know Chinese culture well. If it were used in the title, those readers might lose interest almost immediately. But "1,800-year-old fashion" may arouse the curiosity of readers, both due to antiquity of the particular fashion referenced and the general fascination with fashion that many people have. Finding an intriguing detail or fresh angle to use in your title will instantly boost your essay's appeal.

• 2. Compose an attention-getting introduction.

Your essay's introduction will determine whether your audience will stay interested or not. The thesis statement — the one essential element in your introduction — lets the reader know what the entire essay revolves around.

In Text B, instead of starting the narrative with the "6Ws," the author acknowledges "a need to belong" and describes the spiritual connection to ancient China of a Chinese university student through the practice of Hanfu.

When writing an essay, you, the writer, may order the elements in the way you think will best attract readers. The standard arrangement given in textbooks — introduction with thesis statement, body with supporting details, and conclusion — is merely a guide to help students begin to understand how to logically combine many pieces of information into a coherent whole. So, of course you can put the ending part in front at the very beginning of your story in order to attract readers.

• 3. Support the topic statements with adequate information.

Each body paragraph typically includes a topic sentence, which is often the first sentence in the paragraph and sets the agenda for the entire paragraph. All other sentences in the paragraph support the topic sentence.

In Paragraph G, the author opens with young people having fun at a festival. Then he describes how they have fun. This is a natural, logical, easily understood arrangement used in other paragraphs, with the author's views and observations added as appropriate.

Arranging a narrative essay in chronological order is common. In such an arrangement, each paragraph's topic sentence should contain some kind of "time stamp" — a word or phrase that clearly marks the place in time of that particular paragraph — so that readers may follow the flow of your narration better.

• 4. In the conclusion, highlight the body's major points.

It is common at the end of an essay to summarize the key points from the body. In Text B, the author concludes his essay, echoing the thesis statement of "cultural belongings."

Sometimes, the ending can be left open so that readers can use their imagination and interpret your story in their own ways. If you have some of your own comments and insights that you think could make your narration more meaningful, you can also include those in the ending paragraph.

V Learn to do more

1. Work in a group. Read the sample essay below which is about a foreigner's experience in China and then answer the following questions.

(1) Do you think the title is proper? If not, can you improve it?

____

(2) Can you write a stronger introduction to this essay?

____

(3) In what order does the author share his experience?

____

(4) What is the function of the last paragraph? Do you think it is redundant?

____

(5) Think about a meeting, conference, convention, or other large gathering you have attended. Write a narrative essay detailing why the experience was interesting and unforgettable.

____

Fishing for Shrimp in the Village of Fengpuao

I've lived in Shanghai for several years. My language school decided to put me to the ultimate test: To let me use my Chinese skills in a rural village — all on my own — for two days.

My trip started early in the morning at the Shanghai Hongqiao Station. After two hours on the high-speed train to Ningbo and two more hours in the bus, I arrived at the village. Fengpuao is so small that it isn't even shown on Google Maps, but 2,000 wonderful people live there, next to a lake and forests.

I stayed with my host family for two days, and they were extremely welcoming from the first moment. When I arrived they had already prepared lunch for me, and because I could talk with them well in Chinese, they told me I could call them Mama and Baba.

They told me that they built their house themselves, in which they live with their daughter Eva. She showed me the garden in which small herbs grow, and where chickens and a dog named Leisi walk around freely.

After that, I joined Baba and two of his colleagues who had a car to go to a farm where bay leaf is grown. After trimming bushes and planting new ones, we went to collect our dinner. We walked to a bamboo forest to cut fresh roots, and then we went knee-deep into the lake to fish for fresh shrimp. It was amazing to see up close how it grows and how it's harvested, and it was the freshest food I ever ate.

That evening, friends and family came over. I could speak freely with all the guests, and we laughed, drank *baijiu* and played *mahjong* (although I was no match for these experienced players).

The next day I woke up to the sound of birds tweeting, something I never had in Shanghai, as usually all I hear is traffic. Baba had left at 5:30 to go to a market to buy some food for breakfast, which was also made with freshly laid eggs from the chickens. The rest of the day we worked on the farm again, this time we fertilized the plants.

We returned home and had a short rest, while Mama was already preparing lunch. In the afternoon, Eva and I walked around the lake. From there I could see how clean everything was and how the area depends mostly on agriculture, and we saw animals like insects, little fish and a snake! When we came back to the house, my Chinese parents took me to a traditional gathering together with their friends close to Ningbo City. After that, they went back to Fengpuao and I to Shanghai.

Even though the trip was only two days, it was an amazing time together with my host family, and something I'll never forget: A rare insight into the life of people living in the Chinese countryside and the chance to prove my Chinese skills. And I've really learned how the people in Fengpuao live much closer to nature than we do in Shanghai, and how life in Shanghai isn't the only life in China. In Fengpuao, life runs at a more natural pace. Thanks goes to my host family and to China. I will never forget our time together.

2. As the sample text above describes, life in rural areas and small towns is very different from that in big cities. People may wonder from time to time whether they should live in a small town or a big city. What's your opinion? Suppose you are assigned to write on this topic.

(1) Fill in the chart by listing advantages and disadvantages of living in a small town and of living in a big city.

	Small Town	Big City
Advantages		
Disadvantages		

(2) Then, check if there are any overlapping ideas and eliminate the redundancies. Decide whether you prefer living in a small town or living in a big city, and write a strong introduction stating your position. After that, think about what an attractive title would be. Consider and outline what supporting information you would include in one or more body paragraphs, and then write a solid conclusion based on that outline.

NOTES

图书在版编目（CIP）数据

新时代主题大学英语基础英语写作学生用书 / 马建华，张飞主编 . -- 北京：中国人民大学出版社，2020.6
“十三五”普通高等教育核心规划教材　新时代主题大学英语系列教材
ISBN 978-7-300-28193-3

Ⅰ. ①新…　Ⅱ. ①马… ②张…　Ⅲ. ①英语—写作—高等学校—教材　Ⅳ. ①H319.36

中国版本图书馆 CIP 数据核字（2020）第 095984 号

“十三五”普通高等教育核心规划教材
新时代主题大学英语
主　审　王守仁
总主编　张绍杰　魏承杰
新时代主题大学英语基础英语写作　学生用书
主　编　马建华　张　飞
编　者　王　丽　赵丽娜　赵立书　庞　博
Xinshidai Zhuti Daxue Yingyu Jichu Yingyu Xiezuo Xuesheng Yongshu

出版发行	中国人民大学出版社		
社　　址	北京中关村大街 31 号	**邮政编码**	100080
电　　话	010-62511242（总编室）		010-62511770（质管部）
	010-82501766（邮购部）		010-62514148（门市部）
	010-62515195（发行公司）		010-62515275（盗版举报）
网　　址	http://www.crup.com.cn		
经　　销	新华书店		
印　　刷	天津鑫丰华印务有限公司		
规　　格	210 mm × 285 mm　16 开本	**版　　次**	2020 年 6 月第 1 版
印　　张	10.25	**印　　次**	2023 年 2 月第 2 次印刷
字　　数	220 000	**定　　价**	38.00 元

版权所有　　侵权必究　　印装差错　　负责调换

中国人民大学出版社外语出版分社读者信息反馈表

尊敬的读者：

感谢您购买和使用中国人民大学出版社外语出版分社的 ______________ 一书，我们希望通过这张小小的反馈卡来获得您更多的建议和意见，以改进我们的工作，加强我们双方的沟通和联系。我们期待着能为更多的读者提供更多的好书。

请您填妥下表后，寄回或传真回复我们，对您的支持我们不胜感激！

1. 您是从何种途径得知本书的：

□书店　□网上　□报纸杂志　□朋友推荐

2. 您为什么决定购买本书：

□工作需要　□学习参考　□对本书主题感兴趣　□随便翻翻

3. 您对本书内容的评价是：

□很好　□好　□一般　□差　□很差

4. 您在阅读本书的过程中有没有发现明显的专业及编校错误，如果有，它们是：

____

____

____

5. 您对哪些专业的图书信息比较感兴趣：

____

____

____

6. 如果方便，请提供您的个人信息，以便于我们和您联系（您的个人资料我们将严格保密）：

您供职的单位：______________________________

您教授的课程（教师填写）：______________________

您的通信地址：______________________________

您的电子邮箱：______________________________

请联系我们：贾乐凯　吴振良　黄婷　程子殊　王琼　鞠方安

电话：010-62515580，62515538，62512737，62513265，62515573，62515576

传真：010-62514961

E-mail：jialk@crup.com.cn　wuzl@crup.com.cn　huangt@crup.com.cn　chengzsh@crup.com.cn　crup_wy@163.com　jufa@crup.com.cn

通信地址：北京市海淀区中关村大街甲 59 号文化大厦 15 层　邮编：100872

中国人民大学出版社外语出版分社